Lower End Farm, Great Comberton
The History of a Worcestershire Farm

© Kate Collingwood 2025

The rights of Kate Collingwood to be identified as the authors of this work have been asserted by her in accordance with the Copyright, Designs and Patents Act of 1988.

All rights reserved; no part of this publication may be reproduced, stored in a retrieval system, or transmitted in any form or by any means, electronic, mechanical, photocopying, recording or otherwise without the prior written consent of the publisher or a licence permitting copying in the UK issued by the Copyright Licensing Agency Ltd. www.cla.co.uk

ISBN 978-1-78792-108-5

Book design, layout and production management by Into Print
www.intoprint.net
+44 (0)1604 832149

CONTENTS

INTRODUCTION..5
WRIGHT 6
1   Thomas Wright c1620 - 1675 and his children...8
         Richard Wright 13
2   William Wright 1662+ – 1743 and his children 16
3   Thomas Wright 1703 – 1767 and his children..18
4   William Wright 1753 – 1776..20
SMITH 24
5   Edmund Smith I 1674 – 1728 and his children..26
         John Smith 1702 – 1740 30
         Richard Smith 1709 - 1748 32
         Robert Smith 1712 - 1755...32
         Thomas Smith 1704 - 1776 32
6   Edmund Smith II 1698 – ?..38
7   Edmund Smith III 1727 – 1780 and his children..39
8   Edmund Smith IV 1765-1799 and his children...44
         John Smith 1795 - 1845 45
         John Edmund Smith...47
9   Edmund Smith V 1785-1862 and his children 49
WHILLOCK...52
10   Susannah Whillock 1733-1819 and her children 56
         Thomas Whillock 1767 - 1834...58
         George Whillock 1762 - 1830..59
         Cyprian Whillock 1774 - 1814 59
11   William Whillock 1771 - 1840...61
RICKETTS...66
12   Walter Ricketts 1826 - 1875 67
13   Lucy Ricketts 1831 - 1922 67
HARDY 72
14   John Hardy 1851 – 1935 and his children 74
15   Annie Hardy 1882 – 1970 75
16   Daniel John Hardy 1880 – 1964 78
17   Sibelle Hardy 1914 – 1999..80

COLLINGWOOD 82
18   Kate Collingwood 83
TIMELINE 84
     OTHER HOUSES IN GREAT COMBERTON 92
     ACKNOWLEDGEMENTS..

ILLUSTRATIONS
Wright Family Tree 7
Thomas Wright's signature 1674 9
William Wright's signature 1776 21
Smith Family Tree..25
Extract from 1809 Plan of the Parish of Great Comberton drawn by Thomas Collingridge............28
Monument to Edmund Smith 1859 50
Whillock Family Tree..53
Lower End Farm on the 1809 Plan of the Parish of Great Comberton 54
Lower End Farm on the 1820 Inclosure Award plan..55
1809 Plan of the Parish of Great Comberton 57
Cyprian Whillock's signature 1813..59
Lower End Farm on the 1909-10 Inland Revenue Land Valuation map........................69
Lucy Ricketts outside Lower End Farm possibly around 1890......................................70
Hardy Family Tree 73
Signoretta 75
Lower End Farm on the 1941-1943 Farm Survey map..78
Lower End Farm and Pool House early 1960's..80
Lower End Farm 1997 83
1809 map by Thomas Collingridge 85
Undated map of Lower End..86
1820 Inclosure Award plan 87
1885 Ordnance Survey map..88
Bricks from the barn and cowshed..90
Undated maps of Great Comberton, about 1815
1 Lower End 100
2 Central area of village.. 101
3 Russell Street... 102
4 South end of village 103

INTRODUCTION

I bought Lower End Farm at auction at the Angel in Pershore on 11th December 1997 and moved in on the 18th. The Farmhouse was virtually derelict, the Bothy was a ruin covered in ivy and the Barn was a just a barn disappearing into brambles. It was not registered at the Land Registry so had not been sold since before 1862. The title to the property was a pile of wills and other deeds and over Christmas I traced the ownership back to the 19th century.

The difficulty with the history of houses is that they did not usually have permanent names until recently. The normal description in a deed identifies it by the name of a previous owner, usually states who lived there and details the outbuildings and land attached to some extent. Only rarely does it tell you exactly where it is. Most families used a limited number of christian names so it is easy to get the lineage wrong. The Smiths were particularly guilty of this. There will inevitably be errors in this account therefore, which others may find in the course of future research. I have tried to make clear where there is doubt but there may also be unknown unknowns.

Heartfelt thanks are due to those firms of solicitors who cleared out their archives to the Record Office. I know others simply dumped deeds hundreds of years old. Some records are still held by the owners of the house they relate to, or worse, as in the case of one house in the village, have been taken by someone selling and moving away. These are inaccessible to the general researcher into family history, and do not benefit from the controlled storage at the Hive.

Finally, given the tangled web of relationships between families, I inevitably collected information about other houses in the village and I have added notes on these at the end of the Lower End Farm history so that anyone who wants to delve further might have a starting point. I only looked in detail at deeds which covered families associated with Lower End Farm so there is much more to be unravelled.

Apart from the original documents stored at The Hive in Worcester (reference number prefixed BA in the footnotes) and other record offices, in private hands, and online databases, the information given here comes from three map sources:

The 1809 map by Thomas Collingridge of the entire parish, the purpose of which is to define the extent of the Hanford holdings ahead of Inclosure. It generally shows owners and long-term tenants so is not a reliable indicator of title.

The 1820 Inclosure Award plan and schedule which definitely shows owners of property and the land they have been allocated in exchange for other land in the open fields.

Another sketchier map of the roads and houses in the village which is untitled but probably also by Thomas Collingridge. The large yew in the churchyard was venerable enough to be the only tree shown on the map, and may then have been 500 years old. A pencil note along with its record office number dates this map at 1809 but this is likely to be wrong: it is more likely to date between Cyprian Whillock's death in 1814 as he is not shown as an owner of property, and Susannah Whillock's death in 1819 as she is shown as the owner of part of Lower End Farm. It has been arbitrarily referred to here as 1815.

WRIGHT

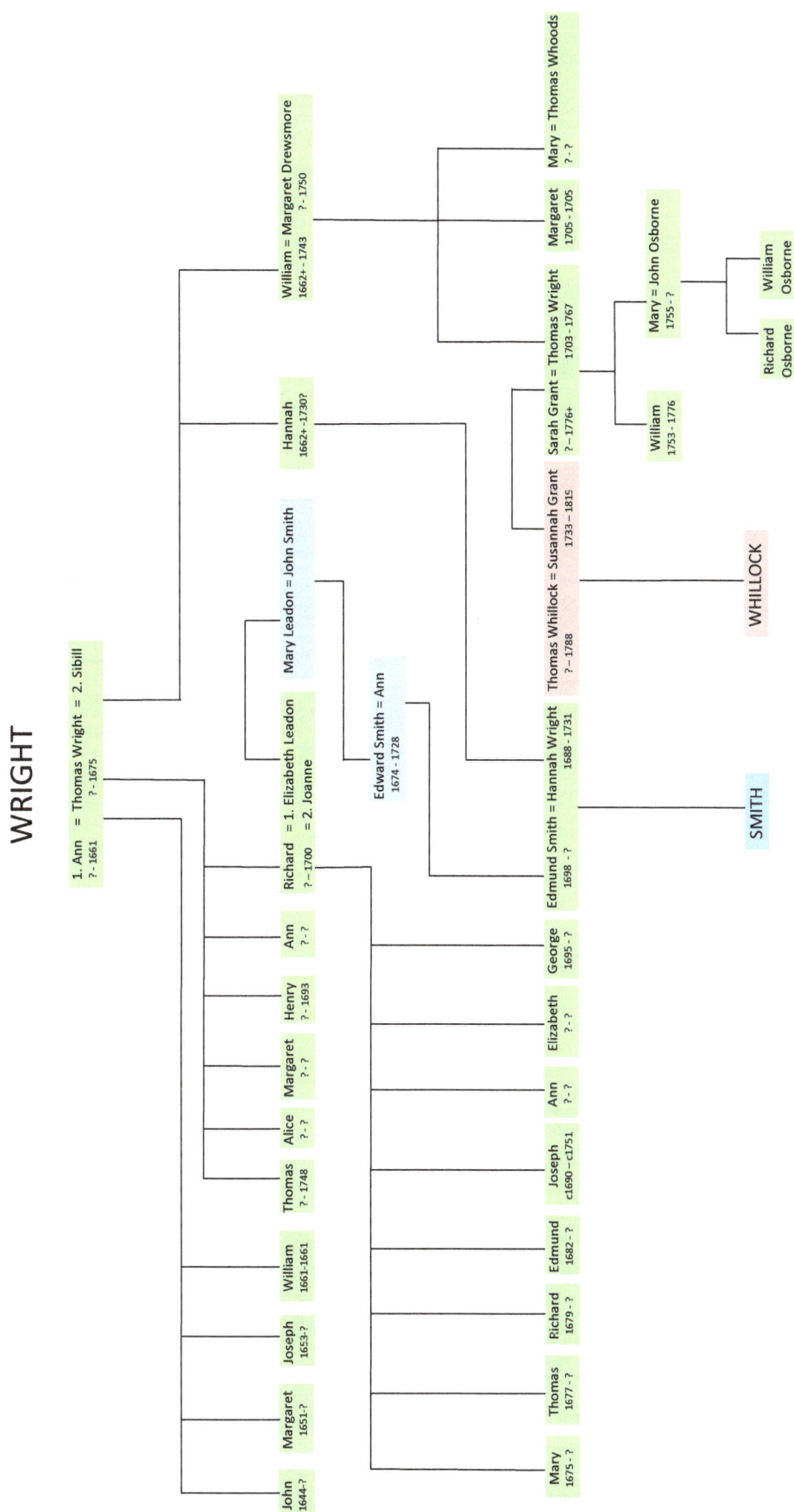

1 Thomas Wright c1620 - 1675 and his children

Thomas Wright died on the 28th November 1675, only 15 years after Charles II returned to the throne following the divisions and depredations of the Civil War and the subsequent Commonwealth. He would have seen the ruins of Pershore Bridge after it was destroyed in 1644 by Charles's army on the way to Worcester, and may even have fought in the war himself. There were about 50 houses in the village at that time, predominantly timber framed with thatched roofs, surrounded by small home closes and orchards and, in the wider landscape, by open fields cultivated in the strips which are still visible in places as ridge and furrow. This number had barely increased by 1871 when Littlebury's Directory records 51 houses, 60 families and a population of 247.

We do not know his date of birth, and therefore his age when he died; for, although the parish records for baptisms extend back to 1541, they are barely legible before the 1690s. His grave is not to be found in the church or the churchyard, maybe eroded away. It was expensive to make a will in the seventeenth century and people would not have wanted to pay for a will that might have needed rewriting if circumstance changed. So the date of a will often tells us something of the state of health of the testator.

Thomas Wright's will was made on the 20th October 1674, and judging by the age of his children; the oldest whose birth was recorded was 31, and two of whom were under 21, he would most likely have been in his early fifties. It is therefore probable that he was in failing health or suffering from an illness that was expected to carry him off before too long, but not mortally sick, as he survived for a further year. He says he is of sound mind and memory, but, unlike other wills, he doesn't mention whether or not he is weak of body. Average life expectancy at birth for English people in the early seventeenth century was just under 40. However, this figure is skewed by the high rate of infant and child mortality: up to 25% of all children born would die in their first year. A man or woman who reached the age of 30 could thus reasonably expect to live to about 60.

Thomas's will includes £12 each to his beloved wife Sibill and his sons William, Thomas, John, Richard and Joseph, and daughter Alice, noting that he has already provided for his now wife and her children though a jointure and has already given his other children as much as he intended them to have out of his estate. It continues:

Item, I give to my said wife eight pounds of lawful english money to be by her employed in the erecting a dwelling house for her to live in upon my ground at or near my barne situate in Great Comberton aforesaid in att or upon the furlong below Tibbis, provided before she receive the said eight pounds she give security by her own bond to my estate hereaforesaid to employ the aforesaid eight pounds to the use aforesaid and not otherwise within one year of my death.

Tibbis was not a building then but a long narrow field stretching north from Russell Street down towards Lower End, and it is reasonable to assume that this bequest was the origin of one of the houses at Lower End. Tibbis was probably named after John Tybbes who was identified in a quitclaim of 1429 or one of his relatives[1]. In 1726 it belonged to the church[2]. An alms board in the church vestry records: *A particular of charities belonging to the parish of Great Comberton in the County and Diocese of Worcester* and includes *one little close called and known by the name of Tibbes* that, along with other land and property is in the possession of John Marriot and Patience his wife, which they held by indenture of lease bearing the date the

---
1 BA950 b705.85
2 BA950 705.85:23

27nd June in the 22nd year of the reign of Charles the Second, ie 1671[3]. It notes that the donor is unknown, and the only surviving feoffee in trust is Edward Walker, *now of Evesham, Attorney at Law*.

Thomas Wright's daughter Hannah received £20 to be paid to her at the age of 21 plus the £10 she was to get from the leasehold lands and his daughter Margaret received £40 to be paid within a year of his death. His daughter Ann was left £10 to be paid at the rate of 50s yearly for four years after his death. Richard was left all his leasehold lands and tenements in the parish of Great Comberton, provided he paid various other legacies. Thomas's household goods were to be valued by two or three *honest and indifferent* neighbours and given to Hannah and Margaret against the money left them. Henry was to be his executor and have the residue of his estate, and in case his son William should die before reaching the age of 21 then Henry would instead inherit *all his freehold lands and tenements which he purchased in fee from any person or persons whatsoever lying and being in Great Comberton*. These had therefore been already turned over to William, probably as Thomas became too ill to run the farm. The will is signed with a thick letter T.

Thomas Wright's signature 1674.

Sibill was Thomas's second wife. His first wife Ann was certainly the mother of John in 1644, Margaret in 1651 and Joseph in 1653, but as there are gaps in the Bishop's Transcripts of the register of baptisms from 1648-50 and 1656-1657, and the Parish register of baptisms is not very clear until the 1690's it is likely that others of Thomas's eleven surviving children were with Ann, given the gaps in their dates of birth. Ann Wright was buried on the 26th February 1661 presumably having never recovered from the birth of her son William who was buried on the 21st February 1661. Thomas's will does refer at one point to *my now wife and her children,* making the distinction to *my other children.* He must have married Sibill sometime after 1661, but neither the marriage nor the births of any of his other children appear in the registers. We can assume William was Sibill's son as he would not have called Ann's son, who died with her, William if there was already one in his family.

The Wright family occur in the Court Rolls of Elmley Castle at various times between 1468 and 1564, and the widow Right is found in a rental schedule of 1627[4] in Great Comberton so they are likely to have been a prominent family locally. Their reputation was not always good. In 1563 Thomas Wright, a butcher, appeared before the manorial court in Elmley Castle charged with selling corrupt meat and the following year he was identified as a common retailer of ale and a common butcher and meat-seller who took excessive profit. John Wright took a lease from the Lord of the Manor of a messuage with appurtenances called Hores in 1469 and Robert Wright appears as a farmer of copyhold land consisting of two closes, 15 acres of arable land and 3 doles of meadow with a cottage in 1557[5].

However, despite a number of exceptionally severe winters in the late seventeenth century, a picture

---

3   Charles II's regnal years are officially counted from the execution of his father Charles I rather than from the Restoration.
4   BA950 b705.85:7
5   Court Rolls of Elmley Castle 1347 – 1564. Ed. Robert K Field, Worcestershire Historical Society 2004.

emerges of the branch of a family on the rise by the time we get to the end of Thomas Wright's life as the inventory of his goods and chattels made after his death by Phillip Sowle, Robert Quarrell, Richard Wright and Anthony Phillips shows. Parts of it are not clear enough to deduce the meaning:

A true Inventory of the goods of Thomas Wright of Comberton magna in the county of Worcester yeoman who departed this naturall life the twenty eight day of November in this present year 1675.

Item	£[6]	s	d
In the Great Chamber			
His money in his … wearing apparrill	6	5	1
2 yards of woolling cloth	0	10	0
Woole malt wheat pots	2	0	0
Meate and butter	1	2	0
Chese	2	0	0
A gyne beadsted with vallians and curtains thereto	1	0	0
A flock bed	0	13	4
3 flock beds more	1	4	0
one feather bolster and pillow	0	8	0
one half head bedsted	0	5	0
One greene blanket and one cradle rugge	0	12	0
Six blankets	1	6	0
One coverlet two curtains	0	7	10
Eight yards of flannings	0	8	0
Three cushings	0	0	9
One pair of flaxen sheets	0	13	6
Eight pair of hempen sheets	2	10	6
a table cloth	0	2	0
Two pillow cass	0	5	0
Three handtowels	0	1	0
Half a duzon napkins	0	3	6
Two tablecloths	0	1	0
One wallit	0	1	0
One pair of old sheets	0	1	0
One male	0	1	0
One gyne chest	0	8	0
One faire cubord	0	1	6
One upholstered chair and stoole	0	2	6
One stoole and two boxes	0	1	0
One cofer and one box	0	2	0
A table straw (?) chair and a forme	0	1	3
A flaskit(?) and a box	0	0	10
Two iron wedgis(?) and a pair shers	0	1	2
	23	6	9

---

6   For the benefit of younger readers £sd refers to pounds, shillings and pence, pre-decimal currency.

In the Hall			
Saucer ….. of …… one …… pott one bason one flagon one porringer one candlestick one salt	1	0	0
The table borde and three joyne stools	0	8	0
The woolling ….	0	1	8
The ….. and a forme	0	2	3
Brass kettles and pots	3	5	0
Iron ware	0	3	5
…… and scales	0	7	0
The spit, brush, smooth iron, our glas	0	3	0
In the Uper Chamber			
One beadstool	0	1	0
A lining ….	0	2	0
A pitch pann	0	1	0
A pair of hand irons	0	1	0
An iron barre	0	1	0
In the Buttry			
Cheese press and frying pann	0	9	4
The meale …. And churne	0	7	0
Three coules and five pailes	0	11	0
Five cheese bats and buter bord	0	3	4
4 sirches one barrill	0	2	4
2 chese ladles one skoope	0	2	0
butter waits	0	0	6
….. ……..	0	2	6
Two lether botes one jack	0	3	6
Three barrels	0	5	4
In the Space(?)			
Four prongs, two hatchits three bills one paire of bellows one iron fire shovel and tongs, one ladel and a spaid	0	9	0
Money at use	140	0	0
A read cow with a store	4	5	0
A read cow with cut tayle	3	0	0
A browne cow	3	10	0
One barren hogg	1	10	0
For hay	5	0	0
For all goods and lumber unpriced above	0	5	0
	156	4	3
Total	179	11	0

It is an interesting insight into the relative values of the day that Sibill would have been expected to build herself a house for little more than twice the value of the brass kettles and pots: this is still an era where goods were expensive and labour cheap. We can see from his will and inventory that his house probably originally conformed to the medieval plan of a hall and a single chamber, or possibly one each side of the hall but which has the addition of an upstairs room that is not used for much other than storage – it appears that all the beds were in the Great Chamber. Cooking was carried on in the hall which indicates the addition of a chimney as otherwise the fire would have been in the centre of the floor with a smoke louvre through the roof.

The family had cows and made cheese and butter, and most likely cider or ale as well judging by the number of barrels. This is the household of a fairly well-to-do yeoman farmer who had been able to take on additional leasehold land in addition to his freehold estate: an indenture of 1663 notes that Thomas Wright was in possession of lands formerly enjoyed by Anne Leadon widow[7]. We can also identify other lands in the possession of Thomas Wright from the counterpart of a lease to Robert Quarrel in 1670 of two ridges lying together in the furlong below Tibbis and the cottage or tenement lately built having the land of Thomas Wright on both sides of the same ridges[8]. This description recurs in property deeds at intervals over a considerable period of time until finally we can identify the cottage as Pool House.

Sibill Wright's burial does not appear in the parish records, we only know that she died before 1704, and we don't know anything about her life as a widow. She may have smoked tobacco: a clay pipe dating from the seventeenth century found in the garden at Lower End Farm could have been hers. Tobacco was certainly being grown in Eckington in 1659 when William George was fined for cultivating 400 poles (about 2.5 acres) of it: growing tobacco in England was illegal as it deprived the exchequer of taxes on imported tobacco. Three of the bells in the church today are dated 1687, the remains of the original set of 5 cast by Matthew Bagley, so she probably heard the beginning of bell ringing in Great Comberton.

Some of Thomas Wright's children continue to appear in the records. His daughter Hannah probably had an illegitimate daughter baptised on the 27th August 1688, also called Hannah – the entry in the baptisms register is difficult to read so we cannot be certain. Also, as we will often find in the course of this story, the habit of families of using a limited number of Christian names makes tracing the line of descent difficult. Five sons might each name one of their sons after their father so that there can be five family members of the same name in a single generation. So when Hannah Wright married Edmund Smith on the 1st August 1726 it is difficult to know if this is the mother or the daughter. The latter seems more likely because their ages would have been closer. The Wrights and the Smiths are intertwined throughout this story and the Smiths have their own chapter later where we will learn more of Edmund and Hannah.

John, Margaret and Ann do not appear again in the Great Comberton records, nor does Thomas's marriage, but he is recorded with his wife Margaret as having a son, also called Thomas, who was baptised in January 1701 and buried on December 16th the same year.

Since his father had been dead for four years this is presumably also the Thomas Wright who was in possession, along with 15 others, of *all that pasture or hilly ground* of Comberton Hill in the nineteenth year of Charles II ie 1679, and also appears in a terrier of rents in 1678 as paying 13s 8d for land in Wicke[9] and

---

7   BA950 705.85:11
8   BA351 705.81:31
9   BA950 705.85:13

in a schedule of rents in 1712 paying 4d for his own land and 14s 4d for land lately Clarkes[10]. Thomas was buried on the 12th June 1748. To confuse the issue, an indenture of 1723 records the surrender by Jonathan Bernards (name not clear) labourer and his wife of the lease of a *cottage and garden grounds near a highway known as Brooke Croft Lane heretofore in the possession of Robert Creese and afterwards in the possession of Margaret Wright widow, also deceased*[11]. Therefore there must also have been another Margaret Wright who doesn't otherwise appear in any surviving records.

Joseph and Richard paid 9s 2d land tax in 1714, so Joseph was still alive then. Henry's signature is on a note recording that the legacies have been paid, on an indenture of 1680[12], and his burial took place on 29th November 1693.

Richard Wright

Richard and William are the only children of Thomas Wright to continue the line to any great extent. Richard married his first wife Elizabeth Leadon about 1670. She was buried on the 8th January 1687. Elizabeth's father Edward Leadon left 1s to each of the children of his son-in-law Richard Wright by his late daughter Elizabeth his wife, naming them as Mary, Thomas, Richard, Joseph and Edmund. Edward's Leadon's will is dated the 5th April 1695 and he died on the 13th April 1695.

Edward Leadon left the bulk of his property to his other daughter Mary, the wife of John Smith of Elmley Castle and then to her son Edmund Smith. Edmund was the father of another Edmund Smith, (who we will call Edmund ll to minimise confusion) that we have already seen marrying Hannah Wright.

The previous year the same Wright children had also benefitted from a legacy from their aunt, Margaret Leadon, spinster and therefore presumably Edward's sister. She left her freelands and meadow grounds in Great Comberton and Eckington to be divided among Mary, Thomas, Richard, Edward and Joseph with her household goods going to Mary and her other goods and chattels to *my kinsman Richard Wright the elder father of the above named children* thus hinting that possibly Richard was a distant relative other than by his marriage to Elizabeth. Her goods and chattels were not extensive, despite her position as a landowner, giving us a glimpse of the life of a spinster:

Atru and perfect inventary of all the goods and chattels of Margaret leadon spincer decesed of comberton magna in the Countie of worsestere

Item	£	s	d
hur weareinge aparill and mounye in hur pocket	2	10	0
In the chamber whear hur died on bed and shetes blankets and all thinges blongings to it	4	0	0
On trunke on cofer on boxe	0	7	0
to ketells on pot to dishise of pouter on frinpone on tabler bourdo on chaire to Joinstollse	1	10	0
All the rest of hur goods un named	0	5	0
tot	8	12	0

---

10   BA950 705.85:18
11   BA950 705.85:22
12   BA950 705.85:15

The Inventory was compiled by Thomas Moore, John Willis and Anthony Whoods, all names which recur throughout this period.

Richard went on to have three more children, George, Elizabeth and Ann with his second wife Joanne. Joanne Wright was buried on the 9th August 1728, so may have been quite a bit younger than Richard who died on the 19th December 1700.

Richard's will, dated the 18th September 1699, was made when he was *in sound and perfect health mind memory and understanding, thanks be given to Almighty God for the same but considering the uncertainty of this life do therefore in the tyme of my health make this my last will and testament*, wisely as it turned out, since he was probably only about fifty but lasted little more than a year afterwards. He left his personal estate to be divided equally between his loving wife and his children, all eight of whom were still alive, and his freehold estate to his son Thomas, out of which he was to pay Richard's debts, and £7 each to his wife and other children. Since the land and property Richard inherited from his father was leasehold he must either have gained the freehold or bought more land in the meantime.

The inventory of Richard Wright's goods and chattels is interesting for comparison with his father's.

Item	£	S	d
In the Chamber where he died			
His wearing apparel and money in his purse	14	10	0
Two beds one chest and two cofers and two chairs and twelve pairs of sheets and other small things	5	0	0
In the Hall			
Ten dishes of pot and two ….. and a ……. one …… pan and two spits and a driping pan and other small things	4	0	0
In the Chamber over the kichin			
One bed and a coffer and a tabell and one forme and other small things	1	7	0
A malt mill and other small things	1	5	0
In the next chamber			
A bed and other small things	1	10	0
In the little chamber			
One bed and a coffer and other small things	0	10	0
In the Dayry House			
Tow hundred of chees and a hanging cupboard and other small things	4	0	0
In the kichin			
Three kettels and three ….. pales and a chees press and two …. and tow pails one gun and a warming pan and other small things	5	0	0

In the Buttry			
Five barrells and a shovl and four bushell of wheat and other small things	1	13	6
A wagon and one long cart and two dung carts and one pair of wheels and tow barrows and three plowes	9	10	0
Three horses and six pair of geares	13	10	0
Eight store piges and tow great pidges	6	0	0
Three store ? and three sheep	10	0	0
Six cowes and tow haifors	18	10	0
Barly in the barns	27	10	0
Wheat in the barns	3	0	0
Hai	10	0	0
The poules	15	0	0
The wheat in the rick	10	0	0
The wheat growing upon the ground	7	10	0
The poultry	0	5	0
The hurdells	0	10	0
The total being	168	18	6

Where Thomas Wright's house was a modification of the medieval pattern, Richard Wright's is of a more modern design with a number of separate rooms, apparently more sparsely furnished, although we cannot tell what is lost to view in the *other small things*. The inventory of farming stock and equipment reveals a flourishing enterprise.

Richard's heir Thomas hardly leaves any trace of his existence. There is a Mary, wife of Thomas Wright, buried on 12th October 1730, and a Thomas Wright buried on 12th June 1748. Four tantalising mentions of a Thomas Wright might lead us to think that life was going all wrong for this Thomas Wright. First there is an entry in a book of Compton Hanford's accounts that in 1716 he rented a house to Thomas Wright and on Lady Day *Wright was indebted to me £1.18.6*[13]

Secondly, an indenture of the first year of George ie 1727 lists:

Ferny close, the barrow or berrow, lowesburrow .... All of which messuages closes, grounds lands and .... Herein before mentioned are lying disposedly in Great Comberton, Wicke and Pensham .... And are now in the tenure or occupation of Thomas Hands as tenant of Edward Hanford at the yearly rent of forty pounds and eighteen shillings or thereabouts and are commonly called or known by the name of Wrights.[14]

Thirdly, an amount of 10s appears in the Parish accounts for 1740 for maintaining Thomas Wright and Elinor Carpenter[15] and lastly, a Thomas Wright appeared before the quarter sessions in 1748:

Be it remembered that on this 24th day of February in the 21st year of his majesty's reign, Thomas Wright of Great Comberton in the said county yeoman was convicted before me (one of his Majesty's Justices of the Board for the said county) of swearing att thirty nine several times thirty nine several profane oaths.

---

13   BA950 705.85:67
14   BA950 705.85:23
15   BA8896 (5) 850

Taken together, this suggests that Thomas Wright may have somehow lost the leasehold lands that his father Richard inherited from his father Thomas, and that this may be why we do not find a will for him or any further record of his life.

Richard Wright's other children also disappear from the record apart for Joseph who died in Abbotts Salford in 1751 presumably without children since in his will dated 26th March 1751[16] he left £5 to his brother Thomas's daughter, sadly for us unnamed, of Great Comberton and the residue to the poor of Great Comberton: this came to £70 18s.

The same alms board in the vestry of Great Comberton church that records the name of Tibbis also details what happened to Joseph's legacy:

Joseph Wright of Abbotts Salford in the County of Warwick and diocese of Worcester Gent left by will the sum of £73.18.0 to the poor of Great Comberton.

This sum it was agreed upon by the Executors of the said Joseph Wright and the Church-wardens and Overseers at a parish Meeting should be laid out in the purchase of a Close or Inclosure called Guildings Meadow containing three acres or thereabouts situate in the Parish of Birlingham and the annual rent thereof applied employed or disposed in and upon the relief support and maintenance of the Poor of Great Comberton by the Minister and Church-wardens of the said parish for the time being for ever 1751 AD

The land was rented out at £5 a year and the proceeds were distributed to the poor annually[17], a practice which survives to this day. Joseph Wright had obviously made something of his share of his inheritances, and classed himself a gentleman where his father and grandfather were styled yeomen. The fact that he left money to his brother Thomas's daughter might bear out the theory that her branch of the family had fallen on hard times and she was more in need of support than the others. It does also tell us that Thomas had married and that at least one of his children survived.

2 William Wright 1662+ – 1743 and his children

William Wright was Thomas Wright senior's principal heir, born sometime after 1662, so he would have been thirteen or younger when his father died, and he inherited the freehold estate. He married Margaret Drewsmore (name not quite legible) in 1699. The marriage does not appear in the records, so we do not know where she was from and it is not a name that occurs in the Great Comberton records. Their first son Thomas was baptised on 16th October 1701 and buried two months later. Their second son, also named Thomas, was baptised in January 1702, which we would now refer to as 1703 since before the introduction of the Gregorian calendar in 1752 the beginning of the New Year was not until 25th March. All dates will be expressed here as Gregorian even when they predate its introduction, as otherwise the chronology is not clear. A daughter Margaret was baptised in 1705, and buried on the 2nd August the same year. The baptism of his daughter Mary is not in the records but we find her marriage to Thomas Whoods in the records of Worcester Cathedral on the 29th February 1733. William was buried on the 4th May 1743 and his wife Margaret on the 4th November 1750.

The 1680's and 90's were one of the coldest times in recorded English history, the peak of what is often referred to as the Little Ice Age. In addition two of the worst storms ever recorded occurred in late October 1694 and the Great Storm of 7 December 1703 which killed between 8,000 and 15,000 people. Despite

---

16   BA9023 850.3.ix:2
17   BA8889 850:7

farming through this period, William seems to have been the success story of the family. We find him in the Parish registers as a churchwarden and constable in 1698 – 9,[18] as a churchwarden in 1714- 1719[19] and 1739, and buying *a piece of pasture ground called by the name of Westcroft.... and also all that one orchard called Duddings .... And one plack of meadow ground lying in the west field called the Bursly plack* in 1716 for £110[20].

In 1742 he acquired the Close on the hill and half an acre in Little Comberton together with *Two butts of land lying in a furlong called Marcroft or Mancroft and one half acre of land shooting down into a place called Over Brooke* on a mortgage for 500 years.[21]

In 1712 he paid rent to the Lord of the Manor of 4d for his own land, 14s 4d for land lately Clarks, 10s 9d for Dobbses, £1 0s 4d for Baylises and 4s 7d for Pallmers.[22] We get some idea of the extent of his landholdings from an undated schedule of rents, probably of 1724:

In the Hill Field of Great or Little Comberton ...... William Wright has 10 ridges .... William Wright hath more in that field viz one ridge in Upper Inchinghill and two ridges in the length below Dead furlong .... Lay field William Wright has 9 ridges .... At a ley of furzes William Wright has 16 ridges ... William Wright hath in the whole of the Dobbs lands 48 ridges.[23]

An indenture dated the 6th November 170[24] confirms that William is Sibill's son, and it echoes the description of the Quarrell lease of 1670:

William Wright of Great Comberton yeoman son and heir male of the body of Sibill, late wife of Thomas Wright, late of Great Comberton yeoman and Margaret wife of the said William Wright to William Wade of Wick ...for £55 ... Two ridges or sellions as above shooting on a close called Tibbes and also the house and barne and outhouses late built and erected on the two sellions or one of them.

A Poll book of electors in 1714 recorded William Wade as living in Great Comberton.[25] Twenty two electors were recorded for Comberton Magna of which sixteen were resident in the village. Other property owners encountered elsewhere in this history were Edmund Nash, Edmund Smith and William Wright. Before 1832 the basic qualification for the vote in county elections was ownership of freehold land worth forty shillings (£2) a year by men aged 21 and over. Until 1774 the man had to reside in the county in which he voted; no woman was eligible. It was said that an income of forty shillings a year made a man independent, being sufficient to furnish him with all the necessaries of life. By 1832 forty shillings would just about support a labouring man for a month.

In his turn, William Wade left *the messuage or tenement wherein I now dwell together with the outhouses, Backside, garden and orchard and all lands thereto belonging which I purchased of William Wright* to his brother Robert in his will dated 24th July 1725.[26]

Overall, it is clear that William Wright was increasing his landholding over a long and prosperous life. His will was dated the 14th October 1740, two and a half years before he died in his early eighties, but sadly it

---

18   BA8896 b850:
19   BA2289 807.9
20   BA351 705.81:2
21   ibid
22   BA950 705.85:18
23   BA351 705.81:28
24   BA351 705.81:74
25   BA13391 b899:1434
26   BA351 705.81:74

is not accompanied by an inventory. He left all his freehold lands, messuages, tenements and hereditaments in Great and Little Comberton to his son Thomas with an annuity of £10 to:

> Margaret my loving wife for and during her natural life at foure Quarterly payments in the year … in full satisfaction of her Dower or right of Dower in or to any of the said lands messuages or tenements and my will is that if my said wife shall at any time claim her Dower in the said premises then that the said Annuity hereby given to her shall cease and determine. I likewise give unto my said wife the use and occupancy of all such household Goods as I had with her in marriage during her life.

In addition, William left an annuity of £8 a year to his daughter Mary, wife of Thomas Whoods from the death of her husband and 12 three-penny loaves to the poor of the Parish on Christmas day. The right of dower meant that his wife would have had the right to take over the farm and its profits for her lifetime, and he wished to avoid this with an annuity.

3 Thomas Wright 1703 – 1767 and his children

Like his cousin Joseph, Thomas Wright styled himself a gentleman, at least after his father's death. As befitted a gentleman, he was married in Worcester Cathedral to Sarah Grant on the 7th April 1750 when he was 47. Grant is another name that does not occur in the Great Comberton registers although they were probably a relatively local family since one of Sarah's sister, Susannah, married a local blacksmith and another, Elizabeth, married William Edgington in Wick on the 20th December 1759. We will hear more of Susannah when we get to the Whillocks.

Thomas and Sarah had two children, William, baptised on the 9th May 1753 and Mary, baptised on the 6th January 1755.

Thomas Wright had inherited his father's lands and property in 1743 and continued to increase, or at least maintain his father's holdings.

In 1757 he was recorded as having lands in Hill Field near Horsley Ditch, Longland, Middle Furlong, Lower Ley, Cross Furlong and Pershore Way together with a messuage with orchard adjoining called by the name of Cartwrights and the orchard called Duddings.[27] He also had rights to the use of common land and paid Common Money for this in 1762[28], and in 1753 he leased Guildings Meadow for a year with Edmund Smith[29].

Thomas Wright's will is dated the 24th July 1766 and he died on the 16th January 1767. He is commemorated by a floorstone in the nave of Great Comberton church which is partly worn away and reads:

> To the memory of Thos Wright Gent who departed ye trancetory life on the 16th day of January 1767 and in the 63rd Year of his Age.
>
> …. was my Life, Strong was my Pain,
>
> …. In Christ is now my gain.
>
> So weep no more my Wife and Children dear
>
> My Joys are great you need not fear

---

27   BA351 705.81:2
28   BA8896 (3) b850
29   BA9023.3 850

It's hoped in Heaven we all shall meet Again

in Bliss and Glory ever to Remain.

Judging by what happened after he died it is doubtful if the reunion in heaven would have been anything other than rancorous.

Thomas Wright's will runs as follows, with the omission of the legal padding:

…… I give and devise unto my dear wife Sarah All those my three messuages or tenements with the Orchard and Appurtenances thereto belonging situate at Wick near Pershore in the said County of Worcester, To hold unto my said Wife and her Assigns for and during the term of her natural Life and from and immediately after her Decease I give and devise my said Messuages Orchard and Appurtenances unto my daughter Mary and her Heirs forever. To my said daughter Mary I also give and devise my Messuage or tenement Orchard and all my Lands with the Appurtenances at North Piddle in the said County of Worcester To hold unto my said daughter Mary and her Heirs forever, Charged and Chargeable nevertheless with the Payment of an Annuity or Yearly Sum of Seven Pounds of lawful Money of Great Britain which I hereby give and bequeath unto my said Wife to be paid for and during the Term of her natural Life at two equal half yearly payments …..I give and devise unto my son William all my Messuages Lands Tenements and Hereditaments situate lying and being at Great Comberton aforesaid, Little Comberton and Eckington in the said County of Worcester To hold unto my said son William and his heirs forever Charged and Chargeable with the Payment of one Annuity or Yearly Sum of Fourteen Pounds of Lawful Money of Great Britain which I hereby give and bequeath to my said Wife to be paid her for the Term of her natural Life……. Which said Annuities of Fourteen Pounds and Seven Pounds before bequeathed to my said Wife, my Will and Meaning is shall be in full clear Recompense and Satisfaction for all such Dower or Thirds as my said Wife shall or may have or claim ….. I also give and Bequeath unto my said Son William and Daughter Mary all and every such Sum or Sums of Money as shall be due or Owing to me at my Death upon any Mortgage, Judgements Bonds or Notes of Hand, to be paid to them in equal Shares as they shall attain the Ages of One and Twenty respectively, and I do direct that the Several shares of my said Son and Daughter in the said Moneys shall be placed out at Interest by my Executors hereafter named until they shall respectively attain such Age and that the Interest and Produce thereof shall be applied in or towards their respective Maintenance and Education ….. and in case the Rent and Profits of my Messuage ad Lands at North Piddle before Devised to my said Daughter shall not be sufficient to pay the said Annuity of Seven Pounds before bequeathed to my said Wife then I do charge and make chargeable my said Daughter's Share in the said Money to be placed out at interest aforesaid with the payment of so much Money to make up the said Annuity ….. I also give and bequeath unto my said son William all and singular the Crop of Corn, Grain, Hay, Impliments of Husbandry and Stock of Cattle which I shall die possessed of. To my said Wife I also give the use of my two best Beds with the Bedsteads, Blanket Sheets and Coverlets thereto belonging and also the Furniture in the Parlour belonging to my dwelling House, for and during the term of her natural Life, and from and immediately after her Decease I give and bequeath the same unto my said Daughter Mary. The Rest of my household Goods I give unto my said Son William, and all the Rest and Residue of my Personal Estate not herein before by me disposed of, after payment of my Just Debts and Funeral Expenses I give and bequeath unto my said Son and Daughter in Manner following (to wit) two third part thereof unto my said Son William, and the other third part unto my Daughter Mary, Provided that in case my said Son and Daughter shall happen to dye within their several minorities unmarried and without Issue lawfully begotten, then I give and devise All my Messuages, Lands, Tenements and Hereditaments whatsoever unto my said Wife and her heirs forever, and in such Case I also give

and bequeath unto her my said Wife, all my Personal Estate whatsoever. And Lastly, I do nominate constitute and appoint my good Friends Thomas Hand and William Phillips, both of Great Comberton aforesaid Yeomen, Guardians of my said Son and Daughter during their respective Minorities, and also joint Executors of this, my last Will and Testament. …..

Mary was twelve when her father died and William was thirteen. The Birlingham parish records include the marriage by banns of *John Osborne of this parish and Mary Wright alias Osborne of the same Parish*. Mary was eighteen when they married on the 9th March 1773, and would have required parental consent; perhaps the alias is a sign that the couple had jumped the gun. It was also normal for a couple to marry in the bride's parish, and taken together the evidence suggests that Mary was keen to escape her childhood home after her father' death. They had two sons, William and Richard.

4 William Wright 1753 – 1776

William Wright does not figure much in any of the archives and the reason quickly becomes clear. He inherited his father's property in 1767, died nine years later aged 22 on the 2? April 1776, and was buried on the 30th April. We need to look at his will, which is dated the 18th April 1776, in detail to understand what followed:

I William Wright of Great Comberton in the County of Worcester yeoman do make publish and declare this my last Will and Testament in manner following, that is to say I give unto my good friend Edmund Smith of Great Comberton aforesaid, fisherman, all my messuage farm and several lands with their appurtenances situate at Great Comberton aforesaid and now in my possession, and also all my Lands with their appurtenances situate at Eckington in the County of Worcester, and now in the Occupation of John Baylis as my Tenant to hold unto the said Edmund Smith and his heirs forever subject to, and I do hereby charge all my Messuage and Lands with the payment of all my just Debts and the several Legacies herein after by me given and bequeathed, to wit, I give and bequeath unto my nephew William Osborne the Sum of Two hundred pounds and to my nephew Richard Osborne the Sum of One hundred pounds, I give and bequeath to my Cousins George, Thomas, Ann, William and Cyprian, Sons and Daughter of Thomas Whillock of Great Comberton aforesaid blacksmith, the sum of Ten pounds apiece, I give and bequeath to each of my Cousins, William and Ann Edgington Son and Daughter of my Aunt Elizabeth Edgington of Wick the sum of Ten pounds, I give and bequeath unto my Servant Girl Sarah Freeman fifty pounds to be paid her (exclusive of her Wages) within six months next after my decease, without interest – I give and bequeath unto my said Aunt Elizabeth Edgington ten pounds to be paid her in one month after my death, and to be at her own disposal without the constraint of her Husband, and I do direct that her Receipt alone not withstanding her Coverture shall be a sufficient discharge to my Executor for the same, and I also direct that the several Legacies herein before by me given and bequeathed to my said Nephews and to my said Cousins the above named Children of the said Thomas Whillock and my Aunt Edgington, shall be paid to them respectively, as and when they shall respectively attain the age of twenty one years with Interest in the meantime, after the rate of four pounds for one hundred pounds by the Year, to be paid to their respective parent or Guardians towards their respective Maintenance or Education. I also give and bequeath to the said Edmund Smith my Ready Money, Stock of Cattle, farm implements of husbandry, Goods Chattels and other my Personal Estate, subject to the payment of all my just Debts, and the several Legacies herein before by me given and bequeathed. And lastly I do nominate constitute and appoint the said Edmund Smith sole Executor of this my last Will and Testament …..

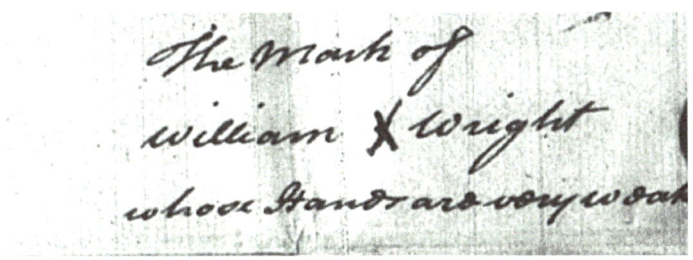

William Wright's signature 1776.

It is signed with an X, the scribe noting that this was *the mark of William Wright whose hands are very weak*. Given that his will was only a few days before his death we can assume that he had either met with an accident, or was suffering from a brief terminal illness.

It is not difficult to imagine how this will was greeted by William's mother and sister. There must have been a major family rift, but whether it was a deathbed whim or a lasting breach is not certain. A certain amount of light is shed on the matter by their next move which was to take legal advice as to whether they could overturn his wishes by questioning his father's will. The draft copy of case for Counsel's Opinion they submitted through Welch of Evesham, Solicitor, still exists but the lawyer's response does not. However, the outcome can be inferred by subsequent wills.

Case upon Mr Thos Wrights Will

Mr Thomas Wright, being seized in Fee Simple of several Messuages and Lands and having by his Will in writing which duly executed and which was attested with such Ceremonies as the law requires for passing lands, and in the words following:

The contents of the will, which we have already seen, is then copied out. The case continues:

The Testator died leaving his sd wife and two children, the son William Wright is lately dead, unmarried, but being a weak young man and given to drinking was influenced by his own Maid and one of his Pot Companions before he died to make a will whereby he has devised the greatest part of his real or personal Estate, worth many thousand pounds to this Companion tho his Mother and Sister are living, and the latter is married and hath Children, and tho he had no reason to be nor in fail ever way unsatisfied with them.

Whether the words in the proviso 'in case my Son and Daughter shall happen to die during their several minorities unmarried and without issue lawfully begotten then' do not narrow the Estate in Fee Simple before devised in the Will to an Estate tail general and in case (?) cross remainders in tail between the Brother and Sister? Or whether the same words with the following 'then I give and devise all my Messuages Lands Tenements and Hereditaments whatsoever unto my said wife and her heirs forever' is not a good limitation of the remainder in Fee to the wife to take effect upon the Sons dying either unmarried or without issue. Vide 'Bowker and Surtees 2 Strange, which seems to be imperfectly reported, and Brownford and Edwards 2 Vezey

2nd If no relief can be had under the above will, what method of proceeding would you advise to call in question and invalidate the Will of Wm Wright the son. Whether a Bill in Equity or an Action in Parliament in the first instance.[30]

Edmund Smith fisherman, the pot companion to whom he left his estate, was the son of Edmund Smith who married Hannah Wright. We know the mother and sister were unsuccessful as Edmund the fisherman owned a property known as Wrights that he stated in his will was left to him by William Wright. They were not so cross that they denied him a tombstone, set in the floor of the church alongside his father's, or perhaps Edmund Smith paid for that. Sadly the verse is worn away as it might have revealed more about him, and the dates are incomplete. The legible part of the stone, next to his father's in the nave of Great Comberton church, simply says: *In Memory of William Wright Gent he departed this life the 2.. day of April 1776 aged … years.*

For some reason he wished his aunt Elizabeth Edgington to have the benefit of his legacy to herself as he exempts it from coverture which is the husband's right to his wife's property.

Sarah Freeman, the servant girl, was 26 at the time, born in Inkberrow. She went on to marry William Salisbury in Little Comberton two years later on the 12th February 1778 and had two sons, Edward and Joseph. Fifty pounds was a substantial legacy, half the price paid for a messuage known as Willis's in 1766.

With the death of William Wright the family disappears from Great Comberton. An assessment for Land Tax in 1798 that lists all the proprietors and occupiers of land in the parish does not include anyone by the name of Wright[31].

---

31   National Archives IR 23/98/108

SMITH

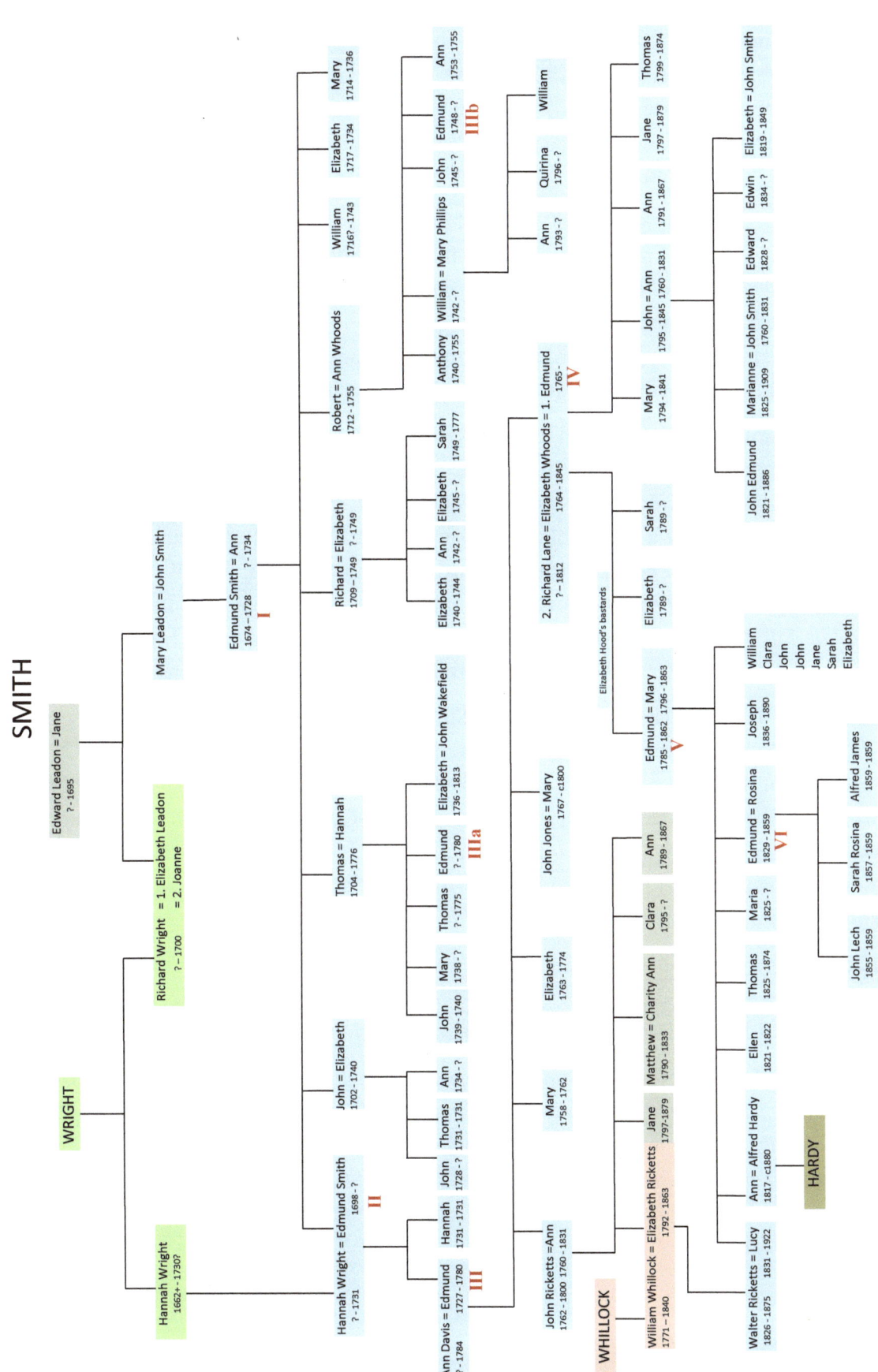

5 Edmund Smith I 1674 – 1728 and his children

Unravelling the Smith family is made difficult by their habit of calling one son in each brood Edmund, so it is not always possible to be certain which is which. The account contains an element of doubt therefore, particularly where the Smiths are active in both Great Comberton and Tewkesbury. To reduce confusion they are numbered here by generation, so John Smith's son is Edmund Smith I, his grandson is Edmund II, and III and IIIa are his great grandsons.

Edmund Smith I was the grandfather of Edmund Smith III, fisherman and companion of William Wright: the *weak young man* who left him the Wright lands and property. He was the son of John Smith of Elmley Castle, and his wife Mary, one of four sons and four daughters. Mary's father, Edward Leadon, left his property in Great Comberton and Birlingham to his grandson Edmund Smith I and his lawful issue, but in case he had none then it would all go to Edmund's brother Thomas. We have already heard about Edward Leadon's other daughter Elizabeth who was the first wife of Richard Wright.

The Leadons had long been established in Great Comberton. In 1523 a Richard Leadon surrendered a messuage called Wexmonsgrounds,[32] and in 1617 he, or another of the same name, was indicted for *breaking and entering on the close of Thomas Dobbs at Comberton called Broad Buckton and consuming the grass thereof with horses and sheep.*[33] In 1637 a Richard Leadon, yeoman, and his son Robert held *right of common for any manner of cattell on Comberton Hill.*[34] In 1681 Richard Leadon (conforming to the custom of using the same name repeatedly within a family) was recorded in a Book of Observations by Walter Hanford as holding *one messuage 2/6d heriott and reliese and one other messuage by ye rent of a red rose. Herriott is most commonly ye best beast.*[35] A heriot was a duty paid to the Lord of the Manor on the death of a tenant.

It is probable that Edward Leadon and Edmund Smith I were working together at least some of the time, as in 1702 Edmund took on fisheries previously shared with his grandfather before he died.[36] Some idea of the yield and value of the Avon fisheries can be gauged by a record of the 326 carp and 440 brace of tench taken from the Woollas Hall fishery 1718, and by the fact that Colonel John Compton Hanford thought it worth employing A. E. St Aubin Weston in 1901 to trawl the Woollas Hall manorial archive of well over a thousand documents to support his claim over the fishing rights in the Avon in a longstanding dispute with Lord Coventry, a job which must have taken years[37].

Edmund I was born about 1674. On the 5th April 1695 his grandfather, Edward Leadon, describing himself as aged and weak in body but of sound mind and memory, made him executor of his will, saying that provided Edmund paid his widow £5 a year in two equal payments:

Then my will is that my said Grandson and his heyres shall hold and enjoy all the said messuage buildings lands tenements free fishings and hereditaments (in Great Comberton aforesaid and in Birlingham) during my said wifes life save only to retain out houseroom for my said wife in the house wherein I now dwell during her life Also I give and devise the reversion …. therein unto my said Grandson Edmund Smith and the heyres of his body lawfully begotten …All of the rest of my goods Cattle Chattells and personall estate I give and bequeathe unto the said Edmund Smith …

---

32 BA950 705.85:1
33 Quarter Sessions 1617.115
34 BA950 705.85:8
35 BA950 705.85:64
36 BA950 705.85:16
37 BA950 705.85:76

Edward Leadon signed the will with a cross, and, as required before 1782, it was accompanied by an inventory:

Item	£	s	d
His wearing Apparell and money in his purse	3	0	0
In the Kitchen ye brass and pewter bason and other small things	2	10	0
In the next Roome one bed and bedstead and other small things	2	10	0
In the Pantry barrels and beere and other small things	1	0	0
In another room a cheesepress and other small things	0	10	0
In ye Chamber one Bed and Bedstead three Coffers	1	0	0
The water and naights ye boat and neets	5	0	0
Five acres of corn growing in the fields	3	5	0
Twenty five Sheep	9	0	0
Total	27	15	0

Apart from the sheep, the fishing rights to the waters and the naights (the small islands in the river of which there were twenty two in the Hanford land), the boats and nets are the most valuable, so Edward Leadon was primarily a fisherman although he was described as a husbandman ie a free tenant farmer or small landowner of lower status than a yeoman. As we would expect from that, he was much less wealthy than Thomas Wright, who predeceased him by 20 years, and his house was more divided into rooms, apparently lacking an upper floor, although ye Chamber might have been upstairs.

Edmund Smith I seems to have been an upstanding member of the community. He served as a churchwarden in 1696 and 1705[38] and as overseer of the poor in 1703.[39]

We can come close to identifying where he lived for the first time as an inventory of land in 1711 in the *Lordship of Cummerton* refers to Birts land lying by Edmund Smith's house.[40] Birts was the field on the south-east corner of Russell Street where it meets Church Street, so he was probably living nearby in Church Street, most likely at the house now known as Longacre which was occupied by his great-great-grandson John Smith at Inclosure in 1820. In 1712 he paid rent to the Manor as a freeholder for a house lately Leadons,[41] in 1713 he is recorded as having rights to the osiers of Ashley ditch and we learn that he was known as Edward or Edmund but more commonly as Ned. In 1714 he was assessed for land tax for his own land and Millcroft, in 1717 he leased osiers.[42] In 1721 he leased *a piece of ground planted with osiers lying at the bottom of a ground called ayotts lying in Great Comberton near the River Avon containing about three quarters of an acre* from Francis Hanford, together with Naights and the Isle of Doggs in Eckington.[43] Osiers are willows coppiced to yield thin flexible rods for basketwork.

---

38   BA2289 807:9
39   BA8896 b850:3
40   BA950 705.85:18
41   BA950 705.85:18
42   BA950 705.85:67
43   BA950 705.85:21

Extract from 1809 Plan of the Parish of Great Comberton drawn by Thomas Collingridge.

Edmund Smith I married Ann around 1696 when he would have been about twenty two. The marriage does not appear in the Great Comberton record so we do not know her maiden name or where she was from. They must have been living in Great Comberton by 22nd April 1697 when their first child, Mary, was baptised, followed by their sons Edmund II on 2nd December 1698, John, baptised on the 11th January 1702, Thomas, baptised on the 24th May 1704, Richard, baptised on the 10th March 1709, Robert, baptised on the 22nd June 1712, and daughters Mary, baptised on the 24th September 1714, and Elizabeth, baptised on the 17th June 1717. William's baptism, about 1716 is missing from the records which are still somewhat erratic at this date, but we can deduce it from Ann's will. The first daughter Mary must have died in childhood before 24th

September 1714 as a second Mary was baptised then.

Edmund died on the 16th August 1728 without making a will, so possibly as the result of an accident. His grave in Great Comberton churchyard confirms his age, and thus his approximate date of birth, and from the inscription he sounds likeable. It reads:

In Memory of Edmund Smith Senior of this parish who departed this life the 16th August Ano Dm 1728 aged 54. A cheerful father and faithful friend he was until his final end.

His widow Ann was granted Letters of Administration to deal with his estate and an inventory of his belongings was made, although, as it does not itemise the contents of each room, it is a less vivid picture of his circumstances. We can see that the house had at least seven rooms and an upper floor; the cider mill seems to have been a separate building. If it is the same house he inherited from Edward Leadon, which only had five rooms, he had been busy with extensions:

Item	£	S	D
Wearing apparel and money in purse	1	10	0
Brass and Pewter with goods in kitchen	4	0	0
In the hall	3	10	0
The Lower chamber	1	10	0
Chamber over the kitchen	1	10	0
Chamber over the hall	2	10	0
In the Cheese chamber	3	0	0
In the Buttery	4	0	0
The Cyder Mill	1	0	0
Corn in the Barn	6	0	0
Sheep and pigs	3	15	0
The horse	4	10	0
2 Cows	5	10	0
Hay	2	10	0
Lease land	8	0	0
Ten tuns of Coal	4	7	6
1 barge	26	0	0
Nett and boats with other materials belonging to the fishery	12	0	0
For rushes	10	10	0
For twig work	3	0	0
Lumber ware	0	10	0
	179	2	6

His widow Ann was buried on the 24th December 1734 and her will dated 15th December 1734 deals with her personal property, the real property having passed to Edmund I's eldest son Edmund II according to the rule of primogeniture which applied in cases of intestacy. By the same rules the widow inherited one third of the deceased's personal property, the rest going to be divided among the children. She left £20 each to Robert, Mary and Elizabeth, £10 to William and Richard and £5 to Thomas and John, the most going to the youngest suggesting that the older children have already benefitted from their father's estate. Edmund, who she refers to as Edward, was left *all those two Closes or orchards with the appurtenances called or known by the name of Calve's Close and the Croft situate lying and being in Great Comberton aforesaid adjoining to the messuage wherein I now dwell together with the Cyder mill and all utensils thereto belonging.*

This gives us a further clue towards pinning down her dwelling since the Croft was a field further up Church Street thus increasing the probability of it being Longacre, as the Croft and Birts bracket that house. Calve's Close is not identified on any map. The cider mill also tallies with the description in Edmund I's will.

Most of Edmund and Ann Smith's children, apart from Thomas, are peripheral to this narrative but because it is not always clear in the archives which person is meant, it will be useful to have a table of them all and their spouses and offspring, before looking at what we can find in the records about each of them:

Edmund II + Hannah Wright	Edmund 1727 – 1780
	Hannah 1731 - 1731
John + Elizabeth	John 1728 - ?
	Thomas 1731 - 1731
	Ann 1734 - ?
Thomas + Hannah	Elizabeth 1736 –c1815
	Mary 1738 - ?
	John 1739 - 1740
	Thomas ? - 1775
	Edmund ? - 1780
Richard + Elizabeth	Elizabeth 1740 - 1744
	Ann 1742 - ?
	Elizabeth 1745 - ?
	Sarah 1749 - 1777
Robert + Ann Whoods	Anthony 1740 - 1754
	William 1742 - ?
	John 1745 - ?
	Edmund 1748 - ?
	Ann 1753 - 1754
William	None known
Mary	None known
Elizabeth	None known

John Smith 1702 – 1740

John Smith was baptised in Great Comberton on 11th January 1702, and little appears in the records to tell us about his life. He died intestate aged 39 and his widow Elizabeth was granted letters of Administration on 9th June 1740. One of the other administrators was Edward Pain.

The Great Comberton parish records show Richard and Anne Pain (Paine or Payne are also used) baptising three children, Sarah in 1698, Elizabeth in 1700 and Anne in 1703, and although Edward's baptism doesn't appear we know of his existence from Richard's will dated 6th September 1731. Edward Pain could therefore have been Elizabeth's brother. We will encounter his son, Richard Pain, later as the first husband of Susannah Grant, before she married Thomas Whillock.

John and Elizabeth had three children, John, baptised in 1728, Thomas, baptised and buried in 1731 and Ann baptised in 1734.

The inventory of John Smith's goods and chattels was signed by Robert Smith, his brother, and William Wright, whose son Thomas married Susannah's sister Sarah Grant in 1750, a further link supporting the theory that Elizabeth Smith and Edward Pain were siblings, and highlighting the intertwined relationships between families in the village.

Item	£	s	d
wearing apparel Money in purse	4	0	0
Goods in the Kitchen Three Brass Kettles one Iron Pott	1	10	0
Five dishes of Pewter and a Dozen of Plates	0	14	0
One Warming Pan and one frying pan	0	01	6
Three Candlesticks one Sconse	0	01	6
Three old Chairs and a Table Board	0	5	0
In the other lower Room four Barrells two Tubs and one Pail	1	0	0
Goods in the Room over the Kitchen one Bed and Bedstead and all as belongs to him and two old Coffers	3	0	0
In the other Chamber a Bed and all as belongs to him and two Chairs	2	0	0
The wood and all other Lumber	1	10	0
	14	02	0

Another Edmund Smith married a woman called Susannah while he was still a minor and also died intestate in 1744. It is likely that he was also John's son judging by the dates: he must have been born about 1725, although no record has been found of his birth, parentage and marriage. The lack of a will normally indicates either an accidental death or a sudden incapacity which rendered the testator unable to communicate since verbal wills, known as nuncupative or nuncup, were also valid until 1838, and appear regularly in the archive. These were testamentary intentions expressed by the decease's word of mouth before credible witnesses', who later made sworn statements before the probate court. By the Statute of Frauds, 1678, there had to be at least three witnesses who had heard the deceased's wishes spoken in his own house and during his last illness. They needed to have them written down within six days, and not proved until 14 days after the death.

Susannah was granted Letters of Administration on the 14th January 1745 in conjunction with Edmund's uncle Thomas, suggesting that his father had died before this date, increasing the probability of his being John's son since John died young in 1740. If this is the case he would have been the eldest son which might account for his probate inventory which shows him occupied with both farming and fishing:

Item	£	s	d
Apparel and money	20	0	0
Brass and pewter	4	10	0
Cheese and Apples	2	0	0
Corn in barn	4	0	0
Fishing net and boats	5	0	0
3 cows and calves 2 heifers	11	2	6
2 pigs	2	10	0
White rods and rushes	5	5	0
Hay rick	3	0	6

White rods are the peeled stems of coppiced osiers for weaving, and rushes were used as a floor covering, either loose or woven as rush mats or other things. There is no record of what happened to Susannah after this.

Richard Smith 1709 - 1748

Richard Smith is another shadowy figure. His christening is recorded on 10th March 1709, he was married to Elizabeth, and the births of their four children are in the Great Comberton registers. His first child, Elizabeth only lived from 1739 to 1742. Ann was baptised in 1742, and a second Elizabeth in 1745. The former may be the Ann Smith who married Andrew Finn widower on the 16th September 1766. Richard was buried on the 25th February 1748 (before the calendar change thus 1749 in today's terms) so his fourth daughter Sarah was born after he died and baptised on the 15th July 1749. Richard's wife Elizabeth was buried on the same evening, leaving seven-year-old Ann, four-year-old Elizabeth and baby Sarah orphans.

Robert Smith 1712 - 1755

Robert Smith also lived in Great Comberton. He married Ann Whoods and their son Anthony was baptised in 1740, William in 1742, John in 1745, Edmund (IIIb) in 1747, and Ann in 1753. Something caused the deaths of his daughter Ann on 14th February, Anthony on 26th February and Robert himself on the 1st April 1755, leaving his wife Ann with three sons under the age of twelve to raise alone. We cannot know whether it was a fire, some form of sickness, or another cause. William went on to marry Mary Phillips and have three children, Ann, baptised in 1793, Quirina (? - the name is only partly legible) in 1796 and William. Robert Smith's grave, just inside the north gate into the churchyard, is one of the few from the 18th century to survive in a mostly legible form. It reads as follows, with his Christian name misspelt and a rather dubious rhyme:

Here lieth the body of Robort Smith who departed this life April the 1 1755 aged 42.

Christ is my life though my body die.

My soul with Christ live happily.

My life's not lost forbare your tears.

My life's not …. Till Christ appears.

Of the last three offspring of Edmund Smith I we get little information from the records. William, Mary and Elizabeth all seem to have died in their twenties or earlier or moved away from the village.

Thomas Smith 1704 - 1776

Thomas Smith was baptised in Great Comberton on the 24th May 1704, and, variously described as a waterman, trowman and bargemaster, he was living and working in Tewkesbury when he died. The Avon was originally made navigable from Tewkesbury to Stratford by William Sandys who was granted permission by Charles I in 1636. It was improved by Andrew Yarrenton from 1664 to allow barges of thirty tonnes to reach Stratford, and by George Perrott in 1758 allowing forty tonne barges to pass. Given the state of the roads at the time, for example the Mary Brook was only bridged in 1755, it is not surprising that we find close links between Tewkesbury and Pershore and the villages along the river. The Stratford Canal didn't open up the route to Birmingham and the east of England until 1816 so trade at this time was limited to the rivers Severn and Avon. The mid-18th century saw the peak of traffic on the Severn, with some 100,000 tons of coal a year coming down from the collieries round Madeley and Broseley to the saltworks at Droitwich and the various riverside towns. Other significant traffic was pig iron from the Forest of Dean and the Ironbridge Gorge, salt from Droitwich, timber coming downriver and the goods needed by the towns going upriver. However, as there were not yet any locks on the Severn, navigation was difficult but lucrative, judging by Thomas's assets when he died.

Although a life interest in a third of Edmund I's estate would have gone to his widow, the rest would have been divided between his children, although, as he had five brothers and two sisters, Thomas's share may not have amounted to much. Edmund Smith II, as the eldest son, was carrying on the family business in Great Comberton, which probably explains Thomas's move to Tewkesbury to establish himself. He may have taken over some of the fisheries from his father in 1729 as, regarding fisheries, Edward Hanford recorded: *received from Thomas Smith and his uncle goodwine on behalf of ye widow Smith*. It would seem that Thomas and his brother Edmund II also co-operated in business as the same ledger records the lease of Ashley Ditch, casting nets and all fish to Thomas in July 1729, then of Ashley Ditch and Laymore osiers to Edmund in 1731, Thomas again in 1732, and Edmund in 1773.[44] He also retained an interest in his lands in Great Comberton as he paid common money here in 1762.[45]

Thomas married Hannah in the early 1730's. Her surname and origin are unknown, but they may have lived in Great Comberton some of the time as their daughter Elizabeth was baptised here on 11th February 1736, followed by Mary on 26th March 1738, John on 6th September 1739, buried on 6th April 1740 and Thomas on 9th September 1742, buried on the 9th July 1746. Mary's death is not in the Great Comberton registers and Thomas and Hannah must have moved permanently to Tewkesbury before he died. His surviving sons Thomas and Edmund's births are also not in the register either in Great Comberton or Tewkesbury although the picture is confused by the existence of another Thomas and Hannah Smith in Tewkesbury in the same period. These could be one and the same although it seems unlikely as the other Tewkesbury Smiths registered the births of six children there, some of which were within nine months of the dates of the children born to the Great Comberton Smiths. It seems likely that Edmund (IIIa) was born soon after their marriage.

The family evidently survived the Great Flood of 1770 in Tewkesbury which must have affected them:

This year produced the greatest flood ever known at Tewkesbury; it was occasioned by an immense fall of snow, succeeded by a heavy rain, which continued without intermission for three days and three nights. On Nov. 17, the water came up St. Mary's Lane and Gander Lane, and united in Church Street; and on the 18th, it rose so high, that boats were necessary in order to pass from the Hop Pole Inn to the Masons Arms. In St. Mary's Lane, the lower stories of the houses were entirely under water, and many of the inhabitants were taken out at the chamber windows, with their beds and furniture. The flood was also in the Church, so that divine service could not be performed. Two houses, near the Mills, were washed down, but no lives were lost.[46]

There were also notable floods in 1763 and 1773 although, living so close to the river, they must have been prepared to a great extent.

Thomas's will is dated June 1773 and, stripped of most of the lawyer's padding, it provides that:

---

44   BA950 705.85:67
45   BA8896 (3) b850
46   Derek Round. Tewkesbury Historical Society

I Thomas Smith of Tewkesbury in the County of Gloucester Bargemaster being weak in Body But of sound Mind Memory and understanding … I Give and Devise unto Edmund Smith of Great Comberton in the County of Worcester Yeoman and William Knott of Beckford in the said County of Gloucester Yeoman their heirs and assigns all and singular my Messuages or Tenements Hereditaments and premises with the appurtenances situate and being at the Key and Key Lane in Tewkesbury aforesaid now in my own possession and in the several occupations of my son Edmund Smith John Moore boatmen and – Griffiths and also all that my Messuage or Tenement Garden Orchard Lands Hereditaments and premises situate lying and being in the parish of Great Comberton in the County of Worcester aforesaid and also all those my lands Tenements hereditaments and premises situate lying and being in the Parish of Eckington in the County of Worcester aforesaid which I bought and purchased of and from Thomas Shepherd and Elizabeth his wife and the Reversion and Reversions Remainder and Remainders Yearly and other rents Issues and profits of the said premises to have and to hold … to the use and behoof of my Dear Wife Hannah Smith and her assigns for and during the term of her natural Life …

and immediately after the demise of my said wife Hannah Smith then as for … my said messuage or tenement hereditaments and premises wherein my said son Edmund Smith now lives in Tewkesbury aforesaid and all those my said Lands Tenements Hereditaments and Premises lying in Eckington aforesaid to the use and behoof of my said son Edmund Smith …

and as for touching and concerning the said Messuage or Tenement Hereditaments and Premises in Tewkesbury aforesaid wherein I now inhabit and dwell and all those my two other Messuages Tenements Hereditaments and Premises with their appurtenances situate lying and being in Key Lane in Tewkesbury aforesaid in the occupations of the said John Moore and – Griffiths to the use and behoof of my son Thomas Smith …

and as for touching and concerning my said Messuage or Tenement Garden Orchard Lands Hereditaments and Premises situate lying and being in Great Comberton aforesaid to the use and behoof of my Daughter Elizabeth Wakefield the wife of John Wakefield of the City of Gloucester Bargemaster …

also I give and Bequeathe unto my said Dear Wife Hannah Smith her executors administrators and assigns all my monies Securities for Money Goods Chattels Effects and Personal Estate of what nature Kind or quality soever or wheresoever to have and to hold the same personal estate … subject nevertheless to the payment of all my just Debts funeral expenses and the charges of proving my will and lastly I do hereby Nominate Constitute and appoint my said Dear Wife Hannah Smith sole Executrix of this my last will and Testament …

The whole will runs to seven pages which must have been lucrative for the lawyer and includes detailed provisions in case anything had happened to Edmund or Thomas in which case their bequest was to pass to their sons in order of seniority and, in the absence of sons, to their daughters as tenants in common not as joint tenants. The different treatment of sons and daughters is common in this period.

Between the date of his will in 1773 and his burial on the 4th September 1776 both Hannah and his son Thomas had died, buried at Tewkesbury Abbey on the 13th January 1774 and the 16th April 1775 respectively. There is a record of the bell at the Abbey being tolled for Thomas on the 10th September at a fee of 2s 6d, and therefore in the afternoon as the fee for the morning was 7s 6d.

A note attached at the end of the will says:

On the seventeenth Day of September in the year of our Lord one thousand seven hundred and seventy six administration with the will annexed of all and singular the Good and Chattels and Credits of Thomas Smith late of Tewkesbury in the County of Gloucester widower deceased was granted to Edmund Smith and Elizabeth Wakefield, wife of John Wakefield the natural and lawful and only children of the said deceased having been first sworn by commission duly to administer, Hannah Smith wife of the said deceased sole executrix and residuary legatee named in the said will dying in the lifetime of the said testator.

Elizabeth and Edmund had thus lost their mother, father and surviving brother in the space of three years. As Edmund and Elizabeth were granted administration of the will themselves there was no need for the services of the trustees named at the start of the will as Edmund Smith yeoman of Great Comberton and William Knott yeoman of Beckford. This Edmund Smith, distinguished in the will from *my son Edmund Smith,* is most likely to be his brother Edmund II, although it could also be Edmund IIIb.

Elizabeth had married John Wakefield, a bargemaster of Gloucester, in Tewkesbury Abbey on the 5th January 1762. They lived in Gloucester, and when he died John Wakefield was described as a gentleman. His grave in the floor of Gloucester Cathedral reads:

In Memory of JOHN WAKEFIELD who died June the 30th 1803 Aged 72 Years. ALSO ELIZth Wife of the above who died Febry 8th 1813 Aged 76 Years.

John Wakefield's will, dated 19th January 1798, does not specify his property in detail, apart from a pasture ground in Barnfield which he left to his son-in-law Richard Burrup and his wife Martha. The remainder was left to his wife to draw the income for her lifetime and afterwards to his son-in-law and daughter, and was unhelpfully described as:

All and singular my other Freehold and Leasehold estates, Messuages and Lands Tenements Hereditaments and premises whatsoever and wheresoever.

Elizabeth Wakefield died intestate and the letters of administration that were granted on the 26th February 1813 read as follows:

On which day appeared personally Elizabeth Cross wife of Charles Cross and alledged that Elizabeth Wakefield of the Parish of Saint Nicholas in the City and Diocese of Gloucester Widow lately died intestate and that the said Elizabeth Cross was and is a Niece and only next of kin of the said deceased – Wherefore she prayed that administration of all and singular the Goods Chattels Rights and Credits of the said deceased might be granted to and committed to her upon giving such good and sufficient security as in this behalf is required ...

Martha must therefore have either been John Wakefield's daughter by a first marriage or both she and Richard Burrup must have died, otherwise they would have been her next-of-kin.

Thomas Smith's son Edmund had been working in partnership with Edward Darke, another bargemaster, but after his father's death the partnership was dissolved and an advertisement in the Oxford Journal of the 14th December confirmed this. The wording suggests a degree of acrimony in the dissolution, and also possibly between Edmund and his father since Thomas sold the boats to Edward Darke rather than leaving them to Edmund:

Tewkesbury November 2nd 1776

Whereas an Advertisement appeared in the Gloucester Journal of October 28th 1776 signed Edmund Smith, intimating, That as the **Partnership between said Edmund Smith and Edward Darke, bargemasters of Tewkesbury,** *was dissolved, the Business would in future be carried on by the said Edmund Smith:-*

> *This is therefore to give Notice That* **EDWARD DARKE, who purchased the Trows of Edmund Smith's father in August 1775, and succeeded him in the said business, and has ever since continued the same (in Partnership with said Edmund Smith)** *will now, on his own account, continue the said Barge Business, with the greatest diligence and punctuality; and his friends and the public may be assured, that all Goods committed to his care will be safely and expeditiously delivered, as he is determined to give general satisfaction to all his employers.*
>
> *Signed EDWARD DARKE*

Thomas Smith's son Edmund (IIIa) is probably the man who married Ann Estop, a widow, on the 13th Nov 1771. They had two daughters, Elizabeth and Hannah before Ann died and was buried on the 12th February 1775. It is unlikely that the children of this union survived as the names were used again for the offspring of his second marriage. Edmund married again, to Judith Cooper on the 14th September 1777 and they had five children. Edmund and Judith were buried on the 25th April and 13th May 1784. On the 10th July 1784 Thomas Cooper stepped forward to adopt the remaining orphans:

> *On which appeared personally Thomas Cooper of the town of Tewkesbury in the County and Diocese of Gloucester whipthongmaker and alledged that Edmund Smith late of Tewkesbury aforesaid Bargemaster and Judith his wife lately died intestate leaving behind them three children namely - Elizabeth Smith aged about four years; Hannah Smith aged about two years and Mary Smith aged about three months and that he the said Thomas Cooper was and is the Uncle and next of kin of the said minors*
>
> *Wherefore he prayed he might be assigned Guardian and Curator at Law to the said three infant children during their minorities upon his giving such good and sufficient security as in this behalf is required and so forth*
>
> *Let the said Thomas Cooper be assigned as Guardian as above prayed.*[47]

This confirms Edmund's marriage to Judith Cooper. It seems either the Quay was not a healthy environment, or Thomas Cooper was not a very good guardian as Edmund and Judith's daughter Elizabeth was the only one to survive into adulthood. She was baptised on the 28th April 1780, and inherited all the Tewkesbury property from her father.

On 20th January 1803, Elizabeth Smith, spinster of Tewkesbury (*only surviving daughter of Edmund Smith of Tewkesbury, barge owner who was the eldest son and heir in law of Thomas Smith*) borrowed £500 from her uncle Thomas Cooper, a whipmaker of Tewkesbury against the Tewkesbury properties on the Quay, described in later indentures as:[48]

> *…messuages or tenements at the Quay and Quay Lane Tewkesbury late in the several occupations of Thomas Smith and Edmund Smith and of John Moore and … Griffiths…*
>
> *…all warehouses on the Quay in Tewkesbury called the Severn Trow and warehouses adjoining and former dwellings in the lower part of Quay Lane…*

As the loan was four days before her marriage, perhaps it was in the nature of a dowry. She married Charles Cross at St Philips in Birmingham on the 24th Jan 1803.

We know that Elizabeth Wakefield inherited the Great Comberton property from her father Thomas. Before the Married Women's Property Act of 1882 all women's real property belonged to their husbands,

---

47 Gloucestershire Archives 1784/98
48 BA12083 899.1208

hence the record that Mr Wakefield paid 3/6 Land Tax in Great Comberton for a property occupied by George Whillock in 1795. Elizabeth and John Wakefield must therefore have given or sold the property in Great Comberton to Elizabeth Cross, perhaps on her marriage, which was only six months before John died, as otherwise it would have passed legally to Richard and Martha Burrup as the heirs to his property in his will if they were still alive.

On Sept 8th 1814 Charles Cross of Tibberton, Gloucestershire and his wife Elizabeth (*late Elizabeth Smith*) borrowed £300 from John Bowyer and the splendidly-named Henry James Window Bowyer, along with Thomas Jordan, rolling in the previous loan from Thomas Cooper and additionally secured on the Great Comberton property which was described as:

Blacksmith shop now in possession of (blank) Whillock... one messuage, one curtilage, one garden 2 acres of land and two acres of pasture in Great Comberton.[49]

The Severn Trow and other properties in Tewkesbury were sold in 1814; an advertisement in the Gloucester Journal of the 26th Sept announced the sale:

Valuable Public House, Store Houses and Premises on the Quay in the Borough of Tewkesbury - to be sold by auction by W. Moore and Son on 5th October 1814 - **The SEVERN TROW** *on the QUAY Tewkesbury*

Lot 1:

All that the said Well accustomed Public House, Store House and Premises, called the SEVERN TROW, now and for many years past in the occupation of Mr John Martin, as Tenant at Will

The premises which are substantially built with brick, consist of:-

On the Basement Floor - of a Cellar

On the Ground Floor - A large Kitchen, Small Kitchen, Parlor, Bar, 2 Pantries and 2 Cellars, detached from which by a Court Yard, wherein is a Pump, are a Brewhouse, Pigstye, and other Conveniences

On the First Floor - are 4 Bedchambers and 3 large Store Rooms

On the Attic Floor - are 2 Bedchambers

Lot 2:

A large pile of Brick Building, formerly used as a Dwelling House, and lately as a Store House, situate on the Quay aforesaid, adjoining the Severn Trow and now in the occupation of Messrs Lloyd & co consisting of:-

On the Ground Floor - 3 Store Rooms, 2 closets, a Shed and a Stable in which is a pump

On the First Floor - 3 Store Rooms

On the Attic Floor - 2 Store Rooms

Lot 3:

A Comfortable Dwelling House situate at the lower part of Quay Lane in the borough of Tewkesbury aforesaid, now in the occupation of Mr Hunt consisting of:-

A Shop, Parlour, Kitchen, Cellar and 4 Bed Chambers

---

49   BA12083 899.1208

On Thomas Cooper's death a year later the Great Comberton property was mortgaged again, described as:

All that messuage or tenement with the blacksmiths shop garden orchard lands hereditaments and premises situate lying and being in the parish of Great Comberton….containing together by estimation 3 acres or thereabout.[50]

Finally, on March 2nd and 3rd 1818, a lease and release from Charles Cross and his wife Elizabeth transferred the property:

Appointment and release of hereditaments and premises in Great Comberton. Charles Cross to William Whillock. George Whillock agrees with Charles Cross for the absolute purchase for £345 but agrees to relinquish the benefit of the contract in favour of William Whillock, the term of 1500 years is assigned to William Whillock and Francis Dinely to be merged in the freehold messuage or tenement with the blacksmith's shop orchard lands hereditaments and premises of 3 acres or thereabouts in the occupation of George Whillock.[51]

We can now identify this positively as the Farmhouse at Lower End Farm as, on the 1815 map of Great Comberton drawn by Thomas Collingridge,[52] it is labelled Wakefield, and in 1820 at Inclosure it was occupied by George Whillock.

There is no clue as to how Thomas Smith acquired the Farmhouse. His nephew Edmund Smith III inherited several properties in April 1776 from William Wright, the *weak young man,* but that is not likely to be the source since Thomas paid common money on property in Great Comberton in 1762, 14 years before William Wright's death. In 1775 an entry in Book no 1252 page 193 of the Woollas Hall records of rent paid by freeholders to the manor has *Owner Smith for Whillock's house*.[53] It is possible that Hannah Wright was given it by her grandmother Sibill or by her uncle William after Sibill's death or on her marriage to Edmund Smith II, and it was then passed by Edmund to his brother, no longer needing it after he inherited the Church Street house from their father. Certainly the brothers were close so this must be a strong possibility.

The difference between the ecclesiastical records in Great Comberton and Tewkesbury is interesting. The latter often includes a cause of death such as scalded to death or drowned by accident, and comments such as, for 1766, *a putrid fever and ye smallpox prevailed very much*. Illegitimate children are noted as spurious or base-born whereas in Great Comberton they are more direct, for example, *the bastard child of Hannah Guryn*.

6 Edmund Smith II 1698 – ?

Edmund II was Edmund I's eldest son and would have inherited his real property at the age of thirty. We already know that he married Thomas Wright's granddaughter Hannah on the 1st August 1726. They had a son Edmund (III) in November 1727, and a daughter Hannah who was baptised on the 4th April 1731. The mother died in childbirth or soon after, and was buried on the 3rd April, leaving Edmund with a three-year-old son and a new baby to raise alone, not very successfully, since the baby was buried on the 27th August 1731. 1731 was not a good year for the Smiths as it was the same year that Edmund's brother John's baby died. There was probably an outbreak of disease, most likely smallpox, typhoid or cholera, in the village that year as there are 9 deaths recorded compared with the normal one or two.

---

50 BA12083 899.1208
51 BA 12083 899.1208
52 BA 445
53 Compiled by A E St Aubyn Weston 1901 BA 950 b705:85 76

He certainly collaborated with his wife's cousin Thomas Wright as an indenture of 1753 records that Edmund Smith yeoman and Thomas Wright, both of Great Comberton leased Guildings Meadow for a year.[54]

Edmund Smith II's burial is not in the parish records, but if he is the Edmund Smith yeoman who was a trustee of his brother's will in 1773 then he lived well into his seventies without leaving any substantial record.

7 Edmund Smith III 1727 – 1780 and his children

This is the Edmund Smith, fisherman, who was the pot companion of William Wright; the *weak young man*, according to William's mother and sister Mary. It is difficult to know if those were just the sentiments of two women who had expected to inherit family assets on William's death and were peeved at being cut out of his will, despite already having inherited substantial property in Wick and North Piddle from his father. Was Edmund a rogue who had deliberately influenced a vulnerable youth for his own ends, or did he simply give William the support he was not getting from his family, and was justifiably rewarded? William Wright did leave substantial legacies to other relatives in his will which perhaps makes us think his ire was solely directed at his mother and sister.

Edmund was 26 years older and so may have been almost a substitute father to William who lost his own father in his early teens. Also, having lost his own mother and only sister when he was three, he understood early bereavement. Edmund doesn't seem to have gone off the rails himself, and the evidence can be interpreted in several ways.

Edmund acted as a churchwarden in 1773 and 1776,[55] which might incline us to look favourably on his character. In 1774 he was commanded to appear before the Barons of the Exchequer at Westminster on 16th May. He was the defendant, along with six other villagers, including John Jones and John Ricketts, in the Bill of Complaint of Griffith Griffiths, Clerk to the Dean and Chapter of the Collegiate Church of St Peter Westminster over a long-running squabble they had with the Hanfords. Both were claiming the lordship of the manor of Great Comberton and thus entitlement to tithes; the dispute was only resolved in 1820 when the Inclosure Award commissioner found in favour of the Hanfords. This is not an indication of illegal behaviour, more a case of taking the side of the local Lord of the Manor against the claims of the church. The register of births has an entry for 9th April 1749 recording the baptism of Elizabeth Smith, the bastard child of Hannah Guryn which could be attributed to Edmund as he was in his early twenties, although, as no Christian name is given for the father, there were a number of other Smiths who could equally have been responsible.

Edmund Smith was baptised in November 1727. He was married in Great Comberton to Ann Davis on the 4th October 1757, and they had five children, Mary, baptised on 23rd July 1758 in a private service, probably because the child was not expected to survive, and indeed she was buried on 14th June 1762, Ann, baptised on 21st Dec 1760, Elizabeth baptised in 1763 and buried on 25th November 1774, Edmund, baptised on 22nd February 1765 and Mary baptised on 5th August 1767.

Edmund Smith, fisherman, was an enthusiastic collector of houses. On 30th September 1749 he bought a messuage with lands from John Moor.[56] Thomas Wright was named in the transaction, possibly as trustee.

---

54 BA9032:3 850
55 BA2289 (9) 807
56 Birmingham City Archive MS3197/284475/284507 and 284517

On 3rd April 1766 he paid £100 for a *messuage tenement or cottage garden orchard and backside now in the possession of Joseph Willis and which he bought of Richard Whittorn*.[57]

A further two messuages known as Clarke's were bought by Robert Stevens of Crowle from Francis Drinkwater, and mortgaged in 1752. Robert left them to his daughter Theodosia Clarke otherwise Goodwin. Following a default on the mortgage it was sold to Edmund Smith on the 7th February 1767 by Thoedosia and her husband John, confusingly named there as John Goodwin alias Clarke.[58]

The details of other properties he bought are recited in an Abstract of Title running to 47 pages describing his grandson John Smith's right to his property.[59] The convoluted nature of these transactions is clear from this document. In 1739 Thomas George of Overbury left land in Great Comberton, along with other land and property in Little Comberton, Bredon and Eckington to his cousin Thomas George Phillips who mortgaged it in 1758 to the Reverend Rowland Bradstock. At the time the land in Great Comberton was tenanted by Edmund Smith and John Cole, and consisted of seven ridges lying together in Brook Furlong, part of Ley Field. By lease and release dated the 4th and 5th July 1766 Thomas George Phillips and his wife, the splendidly-named Colliberry, sold it to Edmund Smith fisherman for £400.[60] A lease and release was a means of transferring property whereby the property was leased for a peppercorn rent to the purchaser and actually transferred by a release the following day. This technicality avoided the need to enrol the transaction, and was thus quicker and cheaper. The mortgage was paid off as part of the purchase money but the term of the mortgage would have endured so we see in property transactions of this time a trustee named who will take over the mortgage term even though there is no money involved any more. In this case it was Edmund's uncle, Thomas Smith waterman of Tewkesbury. Part of the reason John Smith had to produce the Abstract of Title was that Thomas Smith failed to make provision in his will for someone to take over the mortgage term after his death so that legal wrinkle had to be ironed out.

The same Abstract of Title deals with a property Edmund bought from Hands and others. In 1765 Thomas Deaves yeoman and his wife Elizabeth mortgaged various land and properties in Great and Little Comberton and Eckington to Hester Charlotte, widow for £150. In Great Comberton this included a pasture called West Croft and an orchard called Duddings, the Close at the Hill and 22 acres in various ridges of arable land along with two messuages with their gardens and orchards. The mortgage was transferred and increased at intervals through various parties including William Wright and the also-splendidly-named Crysogon Watson at which time the two messuages were owned by William Crees Davis, whose wife was Thomas Deaves's daughter. By 1752 William Crees Davis owed £420 and was joined in the mortgage by his son William. On the 1st and 2nd August 1757, Thomas Hands of Little Comberton yeoman agreed to buy the Great Comberton properties for £1200 less the £350 he had already taken on of the mortgage. He also covenanted to reconvey back to William Davis *a messuage or tenement then lately erected and built by the said Wm Davis on part of the Orchard called Cartwrights (parcel of said premises) together with the garden ground thereto adjoining*. Probate of Thomas Hands's will was proved at Worcester on the 4th May 1774, leaving his property to various relatives. The house went to his brother Robert Hand with the proviso that his beneficiaries should furnish his widow Esther with *sufficient meat drink washing and all other necessaries in the said messuage for her life and if he or they should misbehave to her so that she should be desirous to live*

---

57   BA12083 899:1208
58   BA351.80 705.42
59   BA351.80 705.81
60   Birmingham City Archive MS 3197/284475/284499 and 284506

elsewhere and support herself then they should pay an annuity of £15 on top of a legacy of £300 that he had promised her when they married. She did immediately elect to leave and it seems as if the various Hands could not or would not pay the legacy and annuity, so Edmund Smith stepped in on the 1st May 1779 to buy all the land and property for £1200. In total this consisted of three messuages, four barns, one toft, two dovehouses, two gardens, six orchards and 150 acres of land, 20 acres of meadow, 20 acres of pasture and common of pasture for all manner of cattle in Great Comberton, Little Comberton and Eckington.[61] It is interesting to note in these various transactions that the price of land is much greater in proportion to property than it is today.

These transfers are another instance where we could see the evidence in different ways. Was Edmund swooping in on a family in turmoil to buy property at a bargain price or was he the saviour in a difficult period for them? Either way the Hands family seem to have worked themselves into a position where they could not pay off the mortgages and annuity, in contrast to their status in 1727 when a terrier of the Estate belonging to Edward Hanford lists them as renting the shortest Westcroft,, the Pound Close or Cobblers Close, the two Stockings, Pigsham, Orchards backside, Wrights backside, the Paddock and Palmers Close, Hill Close and Lousborough together with a good deal *of land in ye common fields* of Great Comberton, presumably in addition to the land and property they sold to Edmund Smith.[62]

Thomas Hands's widow Esther went off to live in Little Comberton and, in her will dated the 14th February 1780, gave £20 each to Mary, Esther and Elizabeth Nash, daughters of her nephew Edward Nash of Little Comberton, and £30 to Esther Nash, daughter of Elizabeth Nash widow of Great Comberton, relationship not stated. We will hear more of Esther and Elizabeth Nash when they marry two of the Whillock brothers, but in common with other families, the repeated use of the same names makes it difficult to untangle the relationships.

Vine Cottage has an exceptionally coherent set of original deeds, still in the hands of the property owner, from 1757 when it was:

lately erected on part of an orchard called Cartwrights adjoining and belonging to a messuage or Tenement lately purchased (amongst other Lands) lately purchased by the said Thomas Hand of the said William Davis and William Crees Davis his father.[63]

The description of Vine Cottage entirely tallies with that of the messuage reconveyed to William Davis, and so we can also identify the one bought by Edmund Smith as one on the corner of Church Street and Russell Street which was demolished sometime after 1925 and the site of which is now part of Hand's Orchard, commemorating the downfall of that family.

William Davis's son Thomas left Vine Cottage to his son William. William the son had no children and left everything to his sister Ann Smith's four children. Vine Cottage must have gone to Edmund Smith IV yeoman as we find his oldest, but illegitimate, son Edmund V, a butcher, living there in 1834.

Edmund Smith was also actively engaged in the fishery, for in 1753 he took out a lease for 21 years of the Avon fishery in Pensham, Birlingham, Great Comberton, Eckington and Nafford.[64] This included *Marybrook, which separates the Manors of Pensham and Great Comberton, and including all islands or neights, fruit, osiers,*

---

61 BA351 705.81.2
62 BA950 707.86.23
63 Vine Cottage private deeds
64 BA950 705:85 76

twigs, rushes and reeds. The rent was £18 a year and a good dish of fish in lent – carp, jack or perch worth 5s.

He died on the 17th February and was buried in Great Comberton on the 22nd February 1780. His will, dated the 31st January 1780, names his son Edmund and daughters Ann and Mary. Leaving out the lawyer's waffle[65] it reads:

I give devise and bequeathe unto my dear Wife Ann Smith and my friend Harry Long of Pershore in the County of Worcester Gentleman All that my Messuage or Tenement Garden Hereditaments and premises with the appurtenances thereto belonging (except the Orchard)… in Great Comberton aforesaid known by the name of Willis's and which I purchased … from Joseph Willis late of Great Comberton deceased. And also all those my two Messuages or Tenements Gardens Orchard and premises with the appurtenances thereto … in Great Comberton …. in the several Occupations of Thomas Clements and Benjamin Williams known by the name of Clarks and which I purchased from John Clark. And all that my Messuage or Tenement Farm Lands Orchards Closes Hereditaments and premises with the appurtenances … in Great Comberton and Little Comberton … known by the name of Wrights and which were given unto me in and by the last Will and Testament of William Wright of Great Comberton aforesaid deceased and now in the occupation of Charles Davis … In trust to my said Wife and the said Harry Long … chargeable nevertheless with the payment of my Debts … As to for and concerning one Moity or half part of all and singular the said Messuages or Tenements Farm lands Closes Hereditaments and premises with the appurtenances thereto …. to receive the Rents Issues and Profits thereof until my daughter Ann shall attain the Age of Twenty one years … and immediately after …. to the use and behoof of my said Daughter Ann and her heirs during the term of her natural life …. And immediately after the decease of my said Daughter Ann To the use and behoof of the Issue of the body of my said Daughter Ann lawfully begotten and in default of such Issue then to the use and behoof of my said Daughter Mary Smith …. And immediately after the decease of my said Daughter Mary Smith To the use and behoof of the Issue of the Body of my said daughter Mary lawfully to be begotten and in default of such Issue To the Use and behoof of my son Edmund Smith his heirs and assigns forever. As to for and concerning the other Moity or half part and share of all and singular the said Messuages or Tenements Farm lands Closes Hereditaments and premises with the appurtenances thereto …. to receive the Rents Issues and Profits thereof until my daughter Mary shall attain the Age of Twenty one years … and immediately after …. to the use and behoof of my said Daughter Mary and her heirs during the term of her natural life …. And immediately after the decease of my said Daughter Mary To the use and behoof of the Issue of the body of my said Daughter Mary lawfully begotten and in default of such Issue then to the use and behoof of my said Daughter Ann …. And immediate decease of my said Daughter Ann To the use and behoof of the Issue of the Body of my said daughter Ann lawfully to be begotten and in default of such Issue To the Use and behoof of my son Edmund Smith his heirs and assigns forever. I give devise and bequeathe unto my said Wife Ann Smith All those my Messuages or Tenements Hereditaments and premises with the appurtenances thereto …. In Great Comberton … known by the name of Moores and which I purchased to me and my heirs of John Moor and now in the several Tenures or Occupation of John Whoods and William Finn …. Unto my said wife and her assigns for and during her natural life and from and immediately after her decease I give the last mentioned two Messuages….. unto my said son Edmund Smith his heirs and assigns for ever. I give … all other my Messuages or tenements Farm Lands Hereditaments and premises …not herein before by me particularly given or bequeathed …to the use and behoof of my said son Edmund Smith and his assigns during the term of his natural life… and immediately after the decease of my said son Edmund Smith to the use and behoof of the Issue of the Body of my said son Edmund Smith lawfully issuing and in default of

---

65   Lawyers were paid by the line and consequently wills tend to ramble on

such Issue To the use and behoof of my said daughters Ann and Mary Smith their heirs and assigns forever and they to take as Tenants in Common.... I give unto my said son Edmund Smith all and singular my Implements in Husbandry Boats Fishing nets and all my utensels used with the same boats and nets. To my dear wife Ann I commit the custody and tuition of my said children whom it hath pleased God to bless us with during their respective minorities not doubting but that as she hath approved herself to me to be the best of Wives, she will also approve herself to them as the best of Mothers. And Lastly my express will and meaning is and I do hereby order and appoint that if any difference question or controversy shall be moved arrive or happen between my said Wife and Children or either of them concerning any Gift, bequest or other matter or thing in this my Will given or bequeathed expressed or contained that then no Suit or Suits in Law or Equity or otherwise shall be brought commenced or prosecuted for and concerning the same but the same shall be wholly referred to the award order and determination of the said Harry Long and what he shall order and direct and determine therein shall be binding and conclusive to all and every person and persons herein concerned.

As we have seen with other wills, they do not cover property which has been passed on before the death of the testator, so it is likely that Edmund IV had already taken possession of the house in Church Street. No tenant is named for Willis's so possibly Edmund III was living there. The income from the properties was to be used for the support of his wife and children and any surplus shared equally between them until his children reached majority. Thereafter his son was to pay his widow an annuity of £20 annually. Unlike his uncle Thomas, his will treats sons and daughters equally and he was clearly a fair and loving husband and father, so perhaps the wording of his will shifts the balance in his favour. The dispute over William Wright's will, only four years before his death, seems to have left a mark since he is keen to avoid litigation over his own will.

Edmund's daughter Mary was twelve when her father died and twenty one when she married John Jones, yeoman of Great Comberton on the 23rd September 1788. He was probably baptised on the 31st March 1759 the son of Abraham and Elizabeth, although the record is complicated by the existence of another John Jones of a similar age in the village at this time, and by the fact that neither John Jones is recorded living in one place for very long.

Mary inherited a half share in Willis's, Clarke's and Wright's with her sister Ann, and this led to a profitable period for the lawyers as the three siblings sorted out the various properties to their satisfaction. John and Mary bought Ann's share of Willis's on the 7th November 1798. They borrowed £60 on Willis's from James Cole, and then on the 19th June 1804 they sold it to Richard Lane for £70 of which £60 4s 6d went to James Cole to pay him off. George Best charged them £6 2s 8d for drawing up the last deed.

On the 1815 map of the village, drawn by Thomas Collingridge,[66] Richard Lane is shown in possession of the house now called The Pound and its garden, so we can have reasonable confidence that this was Willis's. The attached orchard was left to Edmund.

On the same map John Jones is also shown in occupation of Pool House and a house which no longer exists on the north corner of Russell Street and Church Street, now part of Hand's Orchard, that Edmund Smith fisherman bought from Thomas Hands, so this was not Willis's.

Mary Jones was buried on the 6th January 1803 survived by John and their four children.

Ann Smith married John Ricketts, a baker of Birlingham on the 2nd June 1788, the same year her sister

---

66   BA445 f9.705.85

married John Jones. It seems likely that John and Ann Ricketts ended up with Clarke's since a pencil note on a later Abstract of John Smith's title states that the deeds for this property are in Mrs Ricketts hands. Given that the 1798 Land Tax Assessment[67] shows John Ricketts and John Jones as the owners of land tenanted by John Woods and that John Whoods was in occupation of Kent's Farm on the 1815 map and Ann Ricketts held it in 1820 it does seem likely that Kent's Farm was Clarke's, Ann having regained her father's legacy after her husband's death. In addition the field immediately north of Kent's Farm was called Kent's Orchard and the one beyond that is called Clarke's Orchard on the 1809 map.

John Ricketts is buried in the churchyard in Great Comberton. His gravestone which is much eroded reads: *Sacred to the memory of John Ricketts who died July 2nd 1800 aged 38 years also Ann wife of John Ricketts who died Jan 6th 1831 aged 79 years.* Ann's baptism is recorded in 1760 which would make her 71 when she died not 79 so there is either a small error on the tombstone or she had lost track of her exact age.

Ann Ricketts exchanged property and land in 1820 as part of the Inclosure Award and numbered 93 on the plan including two cottages gardens and orchards at Upper End, now Back Lane, bounded on the north-west by cottages and gardens of William Whillock and John Tumbrill. This is known here as House A, demolished by Ralph Brookes in the mid-20th century.

John and Ann Ricketts had five children including Elizabeth, born at Nafford Mill and baptised on the 9th January 1792. She returns later when she marries William Whillock. One other of their children, Matthew, who became a farmer at Woollas, and his wife Charity Ann, were the parents of Mary Ricketts who married Joseph Lane.

8 Edmund Smith IV 1765-1799 and his children

Edmund's father, always described as Edmund Smith, fisherman, was buried on his fifteenth birthday. Edmund Smith IV was always called Edmund Smith, yeoman, indicating that his contemporaries were as prone to confusion as we are. He seems to have been more of a farmer than a fisherman, and we know from a 1798 lease that flax, hemp and rape seed were being grown in the parish in addition to the more usual cereals and beans.[68]

He must have inherited the properties in Russell Street and Church Street, now respectively known as Fern Cottage, which his father was given by William Wright, and Longacre, the house passed down from his great-grandfather, and never mentioned in any of the wills, since his son John owned them at Inclosure in 1820. We can also tentatively identify the house known as Moore's as Church Cottage, facing the churchyard on the same side of the road, as this was shown as occupied by William Moore and Mary Finn on Thomas Collingridge's map of the village houses in about 1815.

A number of property transactions occur in the last decade of the eighteenth century. Edmund took out his first mortgage on the Great Comberton properties, and by the time he died he owed Wakeman Long £838, which mortgage was transferred to Lydia Reynolds on the 4th December 1811, long after his death.

Edmund Smith married Elizabeth Whoods at St Andrew's Pershore on the 10th Jan 1792. The Whoods (Hood or Hoods) feature prominently in the history of the village over a long period of time; Edmund's great-uncle Robert had married Ann Whoods about 1740. Edmund and Elizabeth already had three children: Edmund, Elizabeth and Sarah Smith: *Elizabeth Hood's bastards,* who were baptised in a joint service

---

67   National Archives IR 23/98/108
68   BA950 705.85.31

on the 26th April 1789. There is also a record in 1792 that *Edmund Smith is the father of Phoebe Moore's bastard.*[69] This cannot be positively laid at Edmund IV's door but there is no other known Edmund at this date of an age where this would be likely.

Edmund and Elizabeth went on to have five more legitimate children, John baptised 2nd April 1795, Mary baptised 7th February 1794, Ann baptised in 1791, Jane baptised 1797 and Thomas baptised 1799, all of whom survived into adulthood.

Edmund Smith IV died without making a will, so probably in an accident, in December 1799, aged 34. On the 25th May 1802 Elizabeth Smith married Richard Lane in Great Comberton. The possibility that this was Edmund's widow is supported by various pieces of evidence. Richard Lane was in possession of Longacre, Fern Cottage and Pound House on the 1815 map of the village and the house on the corner of Russell Street is marked Lane at Inclosure in 1820, all properties owned by Edmund Smith fisherman. Also Elizabeth Lane was buried among the Smith graves when she died on the 11th December 1845.

When Edmund died Elizabeth was a widow of 35 with eight children between fourteen and six months old and a large farm to run, so it is not surprising she looked for another husband. Before the Married Women's Property Act Elizabeth Smith's property would have belonged to her second husband, but when Richard died in May 1812, leaving her with a further two children, Clarinda and Joseph, the property she brought to the marriage reverted to her in law for her lifetime and then to her oldest legitimate son. Richard's will, dated 17th May 1812 left *all my messuages or tenements gardens or premises situate in Great Comberton now in the several occupations of John Jones to my wife Elizabeth for life and then the messuage occupied by John Jones to my son Joseph and the messuage occupied by William Mann to my daughter Clarinda*. It was witnessed by Thomas Collingridge, Joseph Shelton and Herbert Woodward.

Elizabeth Lane is buried under the great yew in the churchyard and her tombstone reads:

Sacred to the memory of Elizabeth Lane who died December 11th 1845 aged 81 years. And now Lord what is my hope. Truly my hope is even in thee. Psalm 39 Verse 8.

Edmund Smith and Richard Lane's graves are not there but there are two stumps of gravestones nearby which could be theirs.

Richard Lane's son Joseph married Mary Ricketts on the 5th January 1837 in Eckington, and they were identified in the 1841 and 1851 censuses keeping the Coventry Arms in Croome next door to John Hardy with Ann Ricketts, Mary's sister, living with them. This link between Croome and Great Comberton will become evident later. The fact that Joseph moved away from Great Comberton would suggest that he did not, in fact, inherit the property his father left him, although he was buried here next to Elizabeth Lane. His tombstone conveys more than most:

Sacred to the memory of Joseph Lane who died August 29th 1854 aged 49 years. He lived beloved and died lamented. Also Mary widow of the above and wife of James Corbett who died Novr 9th 1862 aged 61 years.

John Smith 1795 - 1845

John Smith was four when his father died. As soon as he reached the age of majority he set out his right to his father's property in three Abstracts of Title extending to 63 pages in total and probably dating from 1817. One begins by ironing out the wrinkles in his grandfather's will in which Thomas Smith was a trustee and

---

69   Quarter Sessions 1792 Easter 529.36

had not named anyone to take his place:

The will of Edmund Smith was proved at Worcester the 7th February 1781. Thomas Smith departed this life many years since ... his wife Hannah died in his lifetime. In 1776 Letters of Administration on the will were granted to Edmund Smith and Elizabeth Wakefield, the only children who since dead and there was not then any legal representative of him and that the said John Smith was then become legally entitled to the freehold and inheritance as eldest son and heir in law of Edmund Smith late of Great Comberton Intestate deceased who was the eldest son and heir in law of the said Edmund Smith fisherman.[70]

The same document continues to say that Edmund and John Wakefield have both departed this life and *the said Elizabeth the widow hath since intermarried with Charles Cross of Tibberton in the county of Gloucester, Gentleman.*

This is particularly interesting as we know from various legal documents already discussed that Elizabeth Wakefield and Elizabeth Cross were aunt and niece, and Elizabeth Wakefield is buried with her husband John. Elizabeth Wakefield had only been dead for about four years so it isn't as if the whole question was lost in the mists of time. As it contradicts the statement in the previous paragraph it would appear to be a simple error.

The whole set of documents deal with the properties his grandfather bought from Clarke, Phillips and Hands, and have previously been discussed in detail. He must have been successful in claiming his grandfather's properties as the Inclosure Award plan has him owning Fern Cottage, Longacre and Pound House. The Lane living on the corner of Russell Street was probably his mother Elizabeth, who had moved and was living in Willis's before 1833 when her daughter Mrs Ricketts paid land tax for *Willis's house where Mrs Lane lives.*

He bought closes named Millcroft and Tedcroft, which was then planted with fruit trees, and a messuage tenement or farm called or known by the name of Hands, and previously in the possession of John Jones as tenant, with barns, stables fold and garden in 1794.

John Smith was recorded in the 1841 census living in Front Street. A John Smith was named as the father of A. Payne's bastard child in 1832 although we cannot be certain this is the same person.[71] He married Ann who came from Elmley Castle and they had seven children, five of whom survived to become adults. John made up for his aberrant name by calling his three sons John Edmund, Edward and Edwin. Two of his daughters, Marianne and Elizabeth, outlived him and two other daughters, Clara and Sarah Sophia, died aged 4 and 14 months respectively. He died in 1845, aged 46, and left the farm, which was subject to a mortgage, to his dear wife Ann for her lifetime so long as she remained unmarried, along with all his ready money and all his stock of beer, cider, perry and other liquors, household stores, wearing apparel and crops. Ann continued the family farm for another eighteen years until she died in 1863 aged 65. She was recorded as a farmer in the 1851 census living with John Edmund, and in 1861 as a farmer of 70 acres employing six men and one boy in Front Street, now called Church Street. John Edmund was 39 and unmarried and Ann's granddaughter Fanny lived with them as a housekeeper with another servant. Ann was buried on the 18th December 1863. After her death the property was to be divided between John's children equally.

John Smith's daughter Elizabeth kindly saved us from further confusion with the wording on her gravestone which reads: *To the memory of Elizabeth Smith wife of John Smith of Birmingham and daughter of*

---

70 BA351 705:81 80
71 BA8896(3) b850

John Smith of this parish who died July 6 1849 aged 30 years.

Marianne also married a John Smith, gentleman of Lyndon End, Birmingham, probably not her sister's widower who was a metal plater, although also from Birmingham. In 1861 the census records John Smith as the owner of land and houses living in Lyndon Green Road Solihull with his wife Mary Ann born in Great Comberton. This predates the 1882 Married Women's Property Act so Marianne's share of her father's estate would still have belonged to her husband.

His son Edward lived at Morton House in Childswickham and is buried in the churchyard there. He must have owned property in the village as in 1896 he provided a water supply to two cottages in Great Comberton.[72]

John Edmund Smith

John Edmund continued the family farm, he's listed in the 1871census as a farmer of 80 acres employing 3 labourers and 1 boy. He was unmarried and lived in Church Street so probably at Longacre with his housekeeper Ann Baylis. By 1881 he had added another boy to the payroll and had Elizabeth Reeve as a general servant.

He is of particular interest because he owned the village brickyard in 1860. This is first recorded in the parish records in 1840 when Bentley's Directory lists Henry Rance as a brickmaker.[73] In 1857 it was operated by J B Baugh,[74] although it is not clear in either case whether they owned it or were the brickmakers employed by someone else. Given that neither name occurs otherwise in the parish records they are more likely to have been employees. The brickyard was located at Plumbden Common which is immediately downstream of the present Quay. No trace of it remains although the steeper section of the bank above the river is cut back below Quay House probably where clay was removed to make the bricks. The Quay only moved to this location after 1820 as it is not shown on the Inclosure Award plan and before 1839 when several landowners got together to try and prevent Quay Lane from being made a public road.[75]

Local brickyards were quite common before the introduction of machine-made bricks in about 1885. Itinerant brickmakers would construct ad-hoc kilns to fire bricks for specific larger buildings and farmers often set up brickworks as they fitted well into the farming calendar. Clay dug in the autumn would be left over winter for the frost to make it more workable, then formed into bricks after lambing and spring planting was finished, and left to dry until after harvest when they could be fired. Stacked in piles and covered in turf or brushwood an entire clamp would be burnt in one go, and this tends to result in an outside layer of overburnt, partially vitrified bricks such as those that can still be seen around the garden of Stowe Cottage, owned at one time by John Edmund Smith and at Lower End Farm where Lucy Ricketts was his first cousin. As rejects these would not have been worth carting any distance and are therefore most likely to be the products of the Great Comberton brickworks.

We do not know how much earlier the brickyard was in operation. Both Lower End Farmhouse and the Bothy are built of hand-made red brick, although the Bothy has a timber frame inside so may have been refaced. Given the difficulty of moving such heavy materials by road in the 17th and 18th centuries a local origin, or somewhere along the river, is more likely.

---

72   BA950 b705.85
73   Bentley's Directory 1840 p67ff
74   BA 850 8889.7
75   BA8896 (3) b850

John Edmund died on the 23rd December 1886. His will is unusually pernickety, perhaps giving us clue as to why he remained unmarried. It is dated the 13th September 1881:

I direct that my body shall be laid beside those of my two deceased sisters near the entrance gate on the north side of the Churchyard of Great Comberton aforesaid and that my funeral shall be conducted in a quiet and orderly manner and that a pall be provided to cover my coffin and a Hatband and Gloves be presented to each person attending my funeral. I also direct my Executor to provide a suitable grave stone to my memory and to defray the cost thereof out of my personal estate. I direct my Executor to pay my Housekeeper Mrs Reeve providing she shall be living with me at the time of my decease her wages for the entire year which shall be current at the time of my decease and to provide her with plain suitable mourning at his discretion the cost thereof to be paid out of my personal estate.

His executor, the hapless Arthur Roberts, farmer of Overbury, was left £10 to cover the trouble he would be put to, which seems slight recompense as there were also numerous bequests to his siblings and other relatives. He did, however fulfil his tasks faithfully as John Edmund's grave is still in excellent condition and in the location required. It reads simply:

In Memory of John Edmund Smith died Decr 23rd 1886 aged 65 years.

Mrs Reeve probably did not benefit greatly either as there were only 8 days left to the end of the year.

John Edmund also owned two freehold cottages known as Pound Row, now known as Stowe Cottage, then occupied by Widow Groves and Charles Freeman, which he left to his brother Edward in the hope that he would keep his grave and those of his parents and sister Elizabeth in a good and proper state of repair. His estate was valued at £1695 net. There is no mention of the family farm.

His exact relationship to each relative he left money to is explained in his will but there is one other substantial bequest to someone who does not seem to be a relative and for which no reason is given:

I bequeathe to my said Trustee the sum of One Hundred Pounds upon trust to invest the same in his name in or upon Government or real securities or in or upon the Debenture Stocks or Preference shares of any Railway or other public Company in England paying at the time of such investment a dividend upon its ordinary stock or shares and from time to time to vary such investments for or into others of the same or a like nature as and when he shall in his sole and uncontrolled discretion think fit and to pay the interests dividends and annual proceeds thereof as and when the sums shall become due and payable to Thomas James of Great Comberton aforesaid for and during the term of his natural life for his absolute use.

The 1881 census shows a Thomas James aged 50 and a carter by trade living with his wife Sarah and a lodger but no children in Russell Street. By 1891 Sarah was a widow.

1891 the census shows that his sister Marianne Smith, widow, had returned to the village as a farmer with her granddaughter Vyvian Hart living with her. Marianne was buried on the 25th July 1909 and her son, John Edward Smith, a solicitor of 9 Bennetts Hill Birmingham finally sold part of the family farm shortly afterwards. We can now finally identify where it was exactly. It was described as:

All that messuage stable coach-house barn shed outbuildings cottage and gardens bounded on the north by Russell Street on the south by land lately sold to Mrs Mingaye and Robert Vines, on the east by land of Mrs Jobling and on the west by Church Street. Four acres three roods and twenty five erches known as Birts, Great Orchard and Orchard but then as Birts Pasture, Orchard, Great Orchard and Cherry Orchard.

This is therefore Fern Cottage which had come down from Thomas Wright through the Smith family. Mrs Anne Maud Elizabeth Mingaye was Marianne's daughter. It is clear from the later censuses that until recently Church Street was known as Front Street and the present main road through the village was Back Street, at least as far as the census returns were concerned.

9 Edmund Smith V 1785-1862 and his children

This is the oldest of Edmund Smith and Elizabeth Whoods's illegitimate children. His grandmother Ann Smith, wife of Edmund Smith fisherman, was the daughter of Thomas Davis who owned Vine Cottage in Russell Street. Edmund's status was never forgotten, an indenture of 1834 refers to him as Edmund Smith otherwise Whoods. Nevertheless, he seems to have been well taken care of, being given Vine Cottage as his share of his father's estate, while his younger, but legitimate, brother John inherited the bulk of the estate.

Edmund V and his wife Mary had 14 children of which two are relevant to this history and will return later: Lucy, baptised on 30th October 1831, who married Walter Ricketts, and inherited Vine Cottage, and Ann who married Alfred Hardy. The family are recorded in the 1841 census:

Edmund Smith 50 butcher

Mary Smith 45

Ellen ? Smith 20

Thomas Smith 15

Hana ? 14

Edmund 11

Lucy 9

William 7

Clary 6

Joseph 4

John 11 months

Edmund Smith V died in 1862 as recorded by his grave in the churchyard:

Sacred to the Memory of Edmund Smith who died June 13th 1862 aged 76 years. Also Mary Smith, wife of the above who died May 2nd 1863 aged 67 years. Blessed are the dead which die in the Lord

His son Joseph became the parish constable and was issued with handcuffs and a staff in 1868, paid for by the churchwardens.[76] His other two surviving sons went to Australia, as did a number of other villagers.

One of these, Edmund, married Rosina Letch on the 7th September 1854 in Collingwood, Victoria.[77] A fine monument in the form of an urn atop a column in Great Comberton churchyard recorded his story and was thankfully transcribed by Walter Davis of Church House before the inscription eroded away, assisted by village lads picking the lead out of the lettering to make fishing weights back in the days when children played outside:

---

76 BA8896 (4) 850
77 https://www.bdm.vic.gov.au/

Monument to Edmund Smith 1859.

This monument was erected by members of the Collingwood Volunteer Fire Brigade, Victoria, Australia in memory of their late Captain Edmund Smith Jnr son of Edmund Smith butcher of this village, who, together with his wife and family were unfortunately drowned in the melancholy wreck of the Royal Charter October 26th 1859 aged respectively

Edmund Smith 30 years

Rosina Smith 23 years

John Lech Smith 4 years

Sarah Rosina Smith 2 years

Alfred James Smith 9 months

When he married Edmund was listed as a carter, and joined the volunteer Fire Brigade soon after its formation in 1856. By 1857 he was the assistant foreman and had risen to foreman by 1863.[78]

The Royal Charter was a 2719 ton iron-hulled three-masted clipper with auxiliary steam engines returning from Melbourne to Liverpool with over 400 passengers and crew. Having made a fast passage, she was caught in a force twelve hurricane. To avoid being driven onto the north coast of Anglesey, the captain put out two anchors and tried to use the engines to hold the ship steady. After an hour and a half the anchor chains gave way and the ship was initially beached on a sandy shore where a heroic crewman managed to get a line ashore to set up a bosun's chair. However the rising tide soon drove her up onto the rocks just north of Moelfre where she broke in two. Those still on the ship were either drowned or dashed to pieces on the rocks by the enormous waves. The ship was bringing many gold miners back to England and while the cargo was insured for £322,000, some of the passengers were carrying gold sewn into their clothes to keep it safe. This did not enhance their buoyancy. Much of the gold was salvaged soon after the wreck but as recently as 2012 a 97gm nugget was found in 5m of water.

Twenty-one passengers and 18 crew were rescued but over 400 souls perished; the final number was never determined as the passenger lists were lost with the ship. The Royal Charter was one of over 100 ships wrecked in one of the fiercest storms of the nineteenth century. On the 19th November 1859 the North Wales Chronicle reported that five bodies were washed ashore, one was a male with 30 sovereigns, 13 shillings, two rings, a piece of foreign coin and a purse with a receipt marked Edwin Smith.[79]

---

78   https://trove.nla.gov.au
79   Holden, Chris and Lesley. Life and Death on the Royal Charter, Calgo publications 2009

WHILLOCK

Lower End Farm

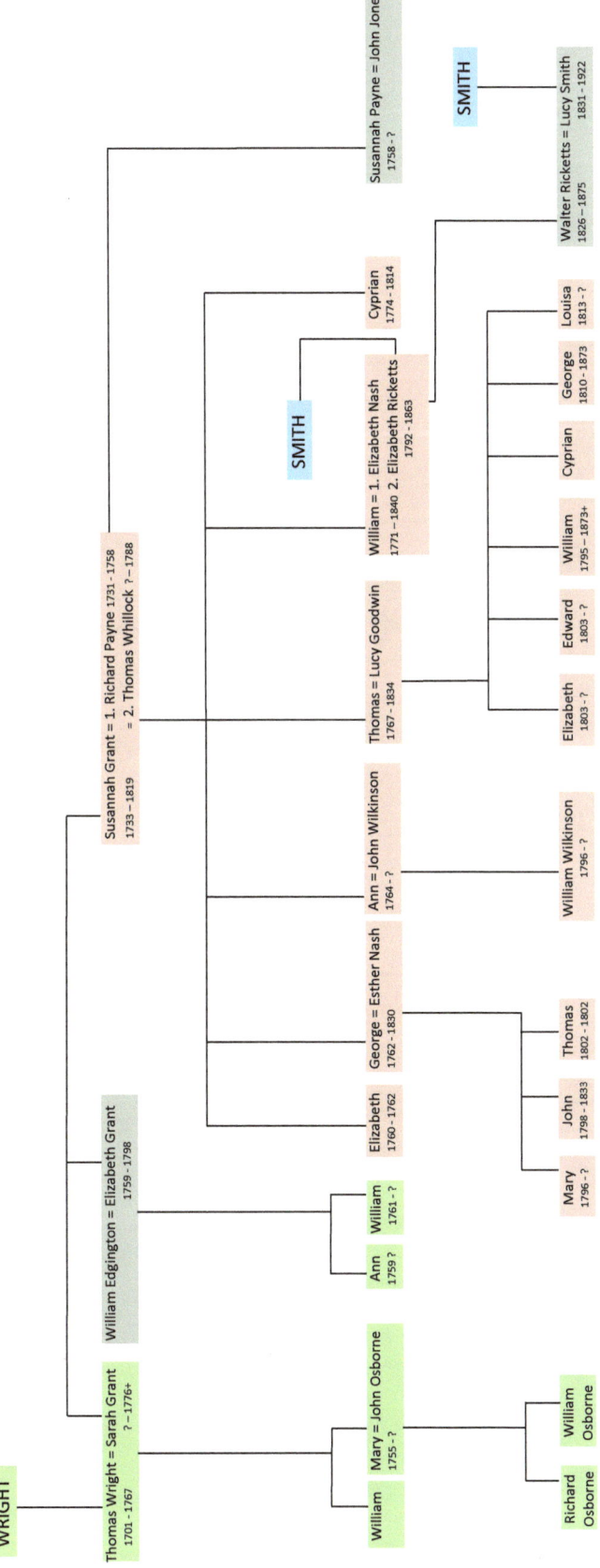

Lower End Farm on the 1809 Plan of the Parish of Great Comberton. Note that south is towards the top of the map.

Lower End Farm on the 1820 Inclosure Award plan.

10 Susannah Whillock 1733-1819 and her children

Nine years after Thomas Wright married Sarah Grant in Worcester cathedral, Sarah's sister Susannah married Richard Payne or Paine, a blacksmith, in Great Comberton on the 10th October 1757. Richard's father Edward, also a blacksmith, who died in 1741, left a will thus:

I Give and bequeath unto Ann my Loving wife all and singular my messuages Lands Tenements and premises lying and being In Great Comberton aforesaid for and during the Terme of her natural Life and also the use of all my household goods and stock in Trade and husbandry to my said wife for her life Provided always and upon this condition that if my said wife shall happen after my decease to intermarry with a second husband that then and from and upon such marriage or death of my said wife which shall first happen I give and bequeath my messuage or tenement in Comberton aforesaid which I now live in and also all my arable lands and premises lying and being in Great Comberton aforesaid to my son Richard Paine and his heirs forever …. Also I give and bequeath (after the death of my said wife or her marriage which shall first happen) unto my son John Paine all that my three parts in four of a messuage or tenement barne stable and garden thereto belonging in Great Comberton aforesaid called or known by the name of Quarrels now in the possession of Richard Wedgewood to hold to my son John and his heirs forever. Also I Give and bequeath after the Death of my said wife all that Barne, Stable Garden Orchard and premises in Comberton aforesaid (except the messuage or tenement) which I latly purchases of John Phillipps unto my said son Richard Paine and his heirs …. and as for and Concerning the messuage or tenement belonging to the said premises last devised I give and bequeathe the same to my son Edward Paine (and also to my said son Edward Paine and his heirs a Close there called Brailes)…. to be pulled downe and carryed off the said premises after the demise of my said wife.

Edward's inventory, listed below, was compiled by William Wright and Edward Whoods, and is almost exactly the same as that of his father Richard who died in 1732:

Item	£	S	D
Wearing apparel and money in Purse	2	0	0
Debts due to the Testator	2	10	0
Goods in the kitchen	0	12	0
In another room below Stairs	0	10	0
In the Room over the kitchen	0	12	0
Cheese	0	7	0
In the same Room one Bed	0	14	0
Shop Goods	1	2	0
Two Cows and two Heifers	4	10	0
One Horse and Hay	3	0	0
Ffourteen Sheep	1	1	0
One Pigg	0	06	0
Lumber Ware	0	2	6
Sum Total	17	6	6

Edward Paine was thus a reasonably well-off small farmer with three houses and land as well as a blacksmith; the shop goods are most likely to be blacksmith's shop equipment, and Richard inherited the business and Edward's house and land. The provision disinheriting his wife should she remarry was important if the testator wished his wife to carry on the business until his children were old enough to take over, since, if she did remarry, the property she inherited from her first husband would automatically belong to her second husband and might then be left to children born to that second union.

Four months after their marriage, Richard died and was buried on the 18th February 1758, probably in an accident, as he left no will. Susannah was already pregnant and gave birth to a daughter, also Susannah, baptised on the 23rd July 1758. The younger Susannah became relatively wealthy at birth as the heir to Richard's messuage and lands, and separate barn, stable garden and orchard. This can probably be identified by the 1820 Inclosure Award plan as a house which no longer exists, one of five on Back Lane which we will call Cottage E. Susannah, the daughter, married John Jones, and a mortgage of the 1st April 1783 confirms this: *John Jones and Susannah his wife only child and heiress of Richard Paine late of Great Comberton blacksmith who died intestate....* Then in 1786 the same property was sold to Mary Stanley, a single woman of the City of London for £197.[80] The other possible alternative location of the property might be Church Gate Cottage and the Old Smithy, since it is the only place in Great Comberton besides Lower End Farm where metal working remains have been found.

1809 Plan of the Parish of Great Comberton.

80   BA950 705.85 52/53

Susannah senior was not a widow for long. On the 14th December 1759 she married Thomas Whillock, another blacksmith, whose family came from Stanway in Gloucestershire, where he was born. Thomas Wright, her brother-in-law, was a witness. This is the first record of the Whillocks in Great Comberton: they were not recorded in a Poll of freeholders in 1714. We do not know if Thomas lived in Great Comberton before he married Susannah or whether he was fetched from Stanway, nor do we know where the couple lived in the early years of their marriage. We can identify properties owned by various Whillocks in 1815 as a tiny building at the east end of Church Cottage, then a separate dwelling but now part of the main house, a cottage at the top end of Back Lane, since demolished, and the cottage known as the Bothy at Lower End Farm. As there is no other record of any sale or transfer of this last and, as it and the barn were shown in the freehold ownership of Susannah Whillock in 1820, it is possible this part of the farm was given to Susannah and Thomas on their marriage by her sister and brother-in-law Thomas and Sarah Wright, and thus didn't form part of the property inherited by the *weak young man* William Wright in 1767, and left by him to Edmund Smith fisherman in 1776.

Thomas and Susannah's children were all baptised in Great Comberton: Elizabeth on 1st May 1760 and buried on the 29th January 1762, George on the 7th July 1762, Ann on the 5th February 1764, Thomas on the 8th May 1767, William on the 3rd October 1771, and Cyprian on the 8th December 1774.

Thomas Whillock was buried on the 4th November 1788. His wife Susannah outlived him by 30 years and was buried on the 7th May 1819 aged 86.

The only likely record for Ann Whillock found was a marriage to John Wilkinson on the 2nd July 1787 at St Marylebone Middlesex, a very grand and beautiful church opposite the south entrance to Regent's Park. They probably had at least one son, William, baptised on the 5th June 1796 at St Lawrence New Hounslow, Brentford. No further information on the Wilkinsons has been found.

Thomas Whillock 1767 - 1834

Thomas Whillock junior was also a blacksmith or shoeing smith. He married Lucy Clarke otherwise Goodwin, the daughter of John Clarke gentleman formerly of Crowle but later of Great Comberton and his wife Theodosia. John and Theodosia sold the property known as Clarke's to Edmund Smith Fisherman in 1767, and John left a life interest in his remaining property to his wife for life and then split between his three daughters in his will dated 19th April 1796.[81]

Thomas and Lucy's first children, William, Mary, and twins Edmund and Elizabeth were baptised in Great Comberton on the 1st February 1795, the 4th September 1796, and the 17th April 1803 respectively. They must then have moved to Tewkesbury as George was baptised there on the 29th April 1810, followed by Louisa on the 13th June 1813 and Margaret Bright on the 24th August 1817. The baptism of his other son Cyprian has not been found. They kept a foot in Great Comberton as their daughter Mary was buried here. Her gravestone reads:

Sacred to the Memory of Mary Whillock daughter of Thomas and Lucy Whillock late of Tewkesbury. She departed this life August 16th 1812 aged 15 years.

Thomas and Lucy moved back to Tewkesbury before he died on 20th November 1834. He owned a house in Barton Street Tewkesbury, shown as a smithy on the south side of Barton Street next to Fletcher's Alley on the 1880 1:500 map of Tewkesbury, as well as a property in Great Comberton, then in the occupation of

---

81   BA351.80 705.43

William Moore as tenant which was the small building at the west end of Church Cottage, and from which he left the rents and profits to his wife. This is probably part of Lucy's inheritance from her father. Thomas and Lucy's son George is listed in the 1841 census as a shoeing smith aged 30 at Fletcher's Alley.

Thomas's will is unusual in that, contrary to normal custom, his wife would continue to receive the profits from his estate even if she remarried, although he specified that his estate should not be liable for any control, debts or engagement of any future husband. After his wife's death the property was to be sold and divided equally between his six remaining children: Margaret Bright must have died in the meantime. The bequests going to his daughters were to be outside the control of their husbands.

George Whillock 1762 - 1830

Susannah's other children George, William and Cyprian stayed in Great Comberton. George married Esther Nash on the 16th July 1795 in Hadzor, Worcestershire. He was also a blacksmith and they had three children, Mary, baptised on 7th August 1796, John, baptised 13th September 1798 and Thomas, baptism unknown but buried as an infant on 10th February 1802. Some of his work is recorded in the parish records: in 1818 he was paid for a wheelbarrow and for rehandling two gravel riddles for sifting material excavated from Town Furlong pit and Lay Pool to be used in resurfacing roads and forming Quay Lane. Smelting slag, nails, hinges, catches and various other items of farm and domestic ironwork have all been found at Lower End Farm, mostly in the area behind the Bothy. George Whillock was buried on the 16th November 1830 aged 72.

Cyprian Whillock 1774 - 1814

Cyprian is the most enigmatic of the Whillocks. He described himself as a Gentleman and when he died aged 40 and was buried on the 21st January 1814, he left a will which read:

All my freehold and personal estate and effects of what nature or kind soever and wheresoever the same may be situate lying and being at the time of my decease and all other my testamentary property of which I may die possessed with their rights members and appurtenances .... Permit and suffer my mother Susannah Whillock and her assigns to have and enjoy the same for and during the term of her natural life and from and immediately after her decease .... Sell and dispose the said freehold and personal estate and effects either by public sale or a private contract for the most money that can be had or gotten for the same .... unto and amongst my brothers George Whillock, Thomas Whillock and William Whillock equally share and share alike ....

His will was dated the 12th October 1813, signed by him in a firm and flowery hand, and witnessed by Matthew Ricketts, John Smith and Francis Dinely. Thomas Collingridge and Thomas Whoods junior were appointed trustees and, on 25th August 1819, when probate was granted to Thomas Collingridge, he noted that the *personal estate of the deceased does not amount in value to £20.*

Cyprian Whillock's signature 1813.

We could easily conclude from this that Cyprian Whillock was subject to delusions of grandeur, until we see, in the 1820 Inclosure Schedule, that the Trustees of Cyprian Whillock were allocated Parcels 32 - Lammas Meadow (originally part of, but now separated from, the field known as Lammas Meadow today, and known now as the Piece or the Ley), 33 - 2 acres, 1 rood and 20 perches[82] in Town Furlong), 35 - Homestead and orchard (the cottage and barn with a small area to the south), 36 - waste (the road verge outside 35), and 38 - Town Furlong (the description is of the section behind the Farmhouse and Pool House although the Plan shows this as Parcel 39). George Whillock was allocated Parcels 38 Homestead and orchard (the Farmhouse and a small area behind), 39 – Town Furlong (the part behind Pool House and the Farmhouse, the same area allocated to the Trustees of Cyprian Whillock as Parcel 38) and 37 – Waste (the verge outside the Farmhouse). William Whillock was allocated Parcels 40 – Homestead (Pool House), 41 – Waste (the verge outside Pool House), 42 - Church Land (a narrow strip east of Pool House) and 34 – Part Orchard, Town Furlong, Lower Orchard 20 perches late belonging to Charles Edward Hanford. These were intended as an equivalent to the lands he owned in the open fields.

Cyprian bought a cottage in Back Lane, described as messuage or tenement, garden and orchard late in the tenure of William Whillock and then of William Spires, on the 20th July 1811 for £373 from Samuel Andrews flaxdresser of Pershore who in turn had bought it from John and Susannah Jones in 1786, and Brailles Orchard, then known as Bryles Close, from them in the same year.[83] This must be one of Edmund Smith's properties, Willis's or Clarke's, identified here as Cottage D. William Spires is shown as its occupier on the 1815 map of village houses, surrounded by Mrs Whillock's orchard.

An indenture of the 28th August 1819[84] details the extent of Cyprian Whillock's property when it was split between his brothers George and William. George and William signed at the bottom and Thomas made a cross as his mark:

All that orchard situate at Great Comberton aforesaid late in the occupation of John Jones but now of the said William Whillock which said orchard was formerly a close called or known by the name of Bryles Close and containing by estimation one acre and a half be the same more or less And also all those several pieces or parcels of arable lying or being dispersedly in the several open or common fields of Great Comberton aforesaid containing by estimation four acres or thereabout be the same more or less and now in the occupation of William Whillock and all which said hereditaments and premises where heretofore bought and purchased by Cyprian Whillock of and from one Samuel Andrews Also all that messuage or tenement situate and being in Great Comberton in the county of Worcester wherein John Jones yeoman formerly dwelt since in the occupation of James Phillips late of the said Cyprian Whillock but now of the said William Whillock And also all that close of pasture ground or orchard adjoining and belonging to the said messuage or tenement containing by estimation one acre or thereabouts be the same more or less late in the tenure or occupation of – but now of the said William Whillock And also all those two ridges situate in a certain common field in Great Comberton aforesaid adjoining to and shooting southward from the end of the said orchard and which last mentioned hereditaments were heretofore bought or purchased of and from Mr James Andrews And also all that messuage or tenement garden and orchard to the same belonging situate and being in Great Comberton aforesaid And also all those pieces or parcels of arable land lying dispersedly in the common fields of Great Comberton aforesaid and containing about four acres be the same more or less which said messuage or tenement was formerly in the

---

82   40 perches = 1 rood, 40 roods = 1 acre
83   BA1926 705.164
84   BA1926 705-164

occupation of Ann Whoods since of the said William Whillock but now of William Sandalls and which said land in now in the occupation of the said William Whillock all which last mentioned hereditaments and premises were heretofore bought and purchased by the said Cyprian Whillock of and from Mrs Ann Moore

From the various maps of the village we can tentatively identify the first of these houses as Pool House which is shown on the 1815 map of the village houses as occupied by John Jones with Jas. Phillips noted next to it, and the second as Bank Cottage which is shown on the same map as occupied by William Sandalls with John Whoods next door.

A note on the back confuses the issue:

Be it remembered that Thomas Whillock of Tewkesbury blacksmith hath purchased from William Whillock the messuage of tenement hereditaments and premises within mentioned to have been purchased by Cyprian Whillock from James Andrews. Indentures of lease and release 30th and 31st inst to Thos Whillock and William Howse. William Whillock covenants to produce documents to prove title.

On the Inclosure Award Plan, George Whillock is shown allocated Parcels 37, 38 and 39 and 42, in other words the Farmhouse and the small area behind it and Pool House, while William Whillock had the Bothy and barn, together with Pool House itself and the remainder of the land.

As the youngest of a large family, we would not normally expect Cyprian to be particularly well off, certainly not by inheritance, and yet he seems to have been the foundation of the family landholdings, by means which are not at all clear. The cause of his death is also unknown. He was dealing in property two years before he made his will which is signed in a firm hand and says nothing about his health. He survived for three months after making his will so it was either an illness or accident which was deemed unsurvivable but not immediately fatal.

11 William Whillock 1771 - 1840

William Whillock married Elizabeth Nash from Little Comberton on the 21st February 1803 by licence in Great Comberton. Elizabeth could possibly have been the sister of George's wife Esther, although the fact that George and Esther married in Hadzor makes it more likely that she was a distant relation. Elizabeth must have died before 1826 without children, since William married again after 1826 to Elizabeth Ricketts, mother of an illegitimate son, Walter. She was born at Nafford Mill, Birlingham and was the daughter of John Ricketts, a baker, and Ann, the daughter of Edmund Smith fisherman, the pot companion and heir of William Wright.

The Ricketts were a large family of farmers based in Birlingham and Woollas in Eckington. Ann and John were married on the 2nd June 1788 and had moved to Great Comberton shortly before the death of her father, since John was recorded as paying rent of £45 a half year to the manor in 1773.[85] Ann Ricketts owned Kent's Farm, along with the orchard which now belongs to Pool House, in 1820; probably part of the estate she inherited from her father.

John Ricketts died intestate on 2nd July 1800, and the letters of Administration for his will are signed by Ann Ricketts and John Jones, husband of her sister Mary. Ann died on 6th January 1831. Their joint tombstone in Great Comberton churchyard reads:

Sacred to the Memory of John Ricketts who died July 2nd 1800 aged 38 years, also Ann, wife of John Ricketts

---

85   BA950 705.85 64

who died January 6th 1831 aged 79 years. The inscription is eroded after this.

Ann's will, dated 6th June 1828, and signed in a firm hand directs her trustees:

All and singular my messuages cottages and other buildings closes lands tenements and hereditaments situate lying and being in the Parish of Great Comberton aforesaid together with all rights members and appurtenances thereto belonging And all my other real estate whatsoever and wheresoever and also all and singular my monies goods chattels and personal estate whatsoever and wheresoever …. Absolutely sell and dispose of my said messuages cottages buildings closes lands tenements hereditaments and real Estate with the appurtenances and the fee simple thereof or any other Estate or Interest I may have therein or any part thereof either by Private Contract or Public Auction …. Shall pay out of the said Sale and other monies to each of my four daughters, Ann, Elizabeth, Jane and Clara the sum of One hundred Pounds apiece for their own respective use and benefit and do and shall pay and divide all the residue of such sale monies rents and profits ready money and debts and monies to be got in and made as aforesaid and all other the said monies and premises respectively unto between and amongst my said four daughters and my son Matthew in equal parts shares and proportions as Tenants in Common and not as joint Tenants and to whom I give and bequeath the same accordingly.

In the ensuing sale in 1833, the orchard next to Pool House was bought by William Whillock to complete the block, as it is recorded in the schedule of Chief Rent for Great Comberton due in 1834 as *Mr Whillock for his part of late Mrs Ricketts's 1/5d.*[86]

He also bought a parcel of Inclosed land called Dobbs Close, which was next to Brailles, from Francis Dinely of Pershore for £180 on the 23rd June 1810, and various lands in the common fields from Joseph Davis in the years leading up to 1820[87] probably planning ahead to maximise his allotment close to home in the Inclosure Award. By 1819 he owed £800 to Charles Bidlake in mortgages.

William Whillock was a churchwarden in 1838[88] and Overseer of the Poor in 1812-13. He lived in either the Bothy or, more likely, Pool House, both of which were his in 1820, and farmed the land he acquired from Cyprian, renting additional grazing land (with the exception of the trees, mines, minerals pits and quarries) in 1823:

William Whillock of Great Comberton, Farmer. Memo of Agreement with C. E. Hanford to take and become a yearly tenant to the said C. E. Hanford from 29th September last past of all those several pieces or parcels of pasture land or ground belonging to the said C. E. Hanford cont'g by admeas't 42a 3r 25p or thereabouts and now in the occupation of the said William Whillock.[89]

A Survey and Particular of the Estates of Charles Edward Hanford Esq carried out by N. Izod in 1820 lists William Whillock as renting a total of 63 acres, 10 roods and 10 perches in Great Comberton.[90]

The mortgage later taken out by Walter Ricketts shows that he also inherited land in Eckington from William Whillock, described as:

All that piece or parcel of pasture or orcharding (formerly consisting of two orchards two pieces of garden land and the site of a messuage) called Row Orchard, containing two acres one rood and nine perches formerly in the tenure of William Whillock and afterwards of John White and sons and now of James Pritchard in

---

86 BA950 705.85 64
87 BA12083 899.1208
88 BA8896(4) 850
89 BA950 705.85 51
90 BA950 705.85 65

Eckington bounded on the north by Oatslay Lane on the south and west by land of John White and on the west by garden land belonging to the parish of Eckington.[91]

William had taken out a mortgage from Charles Bidlake, a druggist of Pershore, for £100 which was added to the £800 he already owed him, presumably, given the date, to finance buying his brothers out of their share of Cyprian's property, and he increased this by a further £59 in 1830.[92] It is not known if he paid off the mortgage.

William Whillock died on 17th December 1840 aged 69 and his will, dated 14th April the same year, reveals his family circumstances:

I give and bequeath unto my niece Mary, the Wife of Matthew Mann of Great Comberton aforesaid the legacy or sum of fifty pounds …. And as to all my money, securities for money, debts due to me, household furniture, farming stock and implements of husbandry and all the rest and residue of my personal estate and effects whatsoever and wheresoever I give and bequeath the same to my dear Wife Elizabeth Whillock to and for her own use and benefit …. All and singular my messuages, lands, tenements and hereditaments situate in Great Comberton aforesaid and at Eckington in the County of Worcester …. To permit and suffer my said Wife and her assigns to occupy possess and enjoy the same or receive and take the rents dues and profits thereof for and during the term of her natural life for her own sole use and benefit if she shall so long remain my widow and unmarried but not otherwise …. and immediately after her decease or next marriage of my said wife whichever shall first happen In Trust for and for the only benefit of her Son Walter Ricketts born before her marriage with me and who is now living with me and aged about Fourteen years and two months for and during the term of his natural life without impeachment of waste except in pulling down and destroying buildings. And from and after his decease or other some determination of his said life estate In Trust for the heirs of the body of the said Walter Ricketts lawfully begotten But in case the said Walter Ricketts shall depart this life without leaving lawful issue of his Body him surviving then In Trust for my Nephew William Wilkinson, his heirs and assigns for ever and to whom I give and devise the same accordingly to and for his and their own absolute use benefit and disposal ….

Walter Ricketts is recorded in the Birlingham Bastardy Orders as Elizabeth Ricketts' son, baptised on 24th February 1826, with no indication as to who the father might have been. Although Walter did indeed die without issue, neither William Wilkinson nor his heirs ever came forward to collect his inheritance, so presumably he had died before Walter, or perhaps, in the intervening 35 years, the bequest had been forgotten, or even deliberately suppressed.

The census in 1841 has Elizabeth and Walter in one household and Esther Whillock next door, George having died in 1830. In 1851 the more detailed census lists Elizabeth as widow, farmer of 14 acres and Walter as her son employed at home, Esther Whillock having died in 1843 at the ripe old age of 93. The Highway Tax assessment in the same year shows that Elizabeth occupied the larger property paying for a house and land, and Walter had a cottage and garden.[93] She was actively running the farm, and certainly making cider for the Worcester Chronicle reported on 23rd April 1856 that she had been charged with selling one gallon of cider to William Godfrey without a licence to do so. William said he sent Sarah Fewtrill and Esther Mann to the defendant's residence on the evening in question for a gallon of cider, giving Sarah Fewtrill one shilling. She returned with the cider in a bottle giving him 2d change and stating that Mrs Whillock had charged 10d

---

91   BA12083 899.1208
92   BA12083 899.1208
93   BA8896(6) 850

for the cider. Sarah Futrill and Louisa Mann stated that Mrs Whillock gave them the cider and told them to keep the money, that they took the bottle to Godfrey's and all of them adjourned to Fewtrill's residence where, assisted by other friends they consumed the bottle of "Godfrey's Cordial" between them but admitted that during the whole evening they said nothing to Godfrey about the 10d nor had they returned it to him. The bench was of the opinion that it was a lame attempt to evade the law and they fined Elizabeth Whillock £2. She was represented by Mr Eades of Evesham whose task was made more difficult by having to defend a woman from Little Comberton of selling cider to William Godfrey two days later.

By 1861 Elizabeth is listed as a landed proprietor, and Walter was head of his own household and a farmer of 13 acres of pasture land with his wife Lucy whom he had married in Worcester Cathedral in December 1857. Lucy was the daughter of Edmund Smith the butcher who lived at Vine Cottage, one of Elizabeth Hood's bastards, making her Walter's second cousin on the wrong side of the blanket. She was also the sister of Edmund Smith who died in the wreck of the Royal Charter.

Elizabeth Whillock was buried on the 28th October 1863 aged 74, and one of the two dwellings at Lower End Farm was listed as unoccupied in the next census in 1871. Walter is described as a farmer of 10 acres and Lucy as his wife.

RICKETTS

12 Walter Ricketts 1826 - 1875

Walter Ricketts comes across as a rather sad character. This may be because the earliest surviving photograph of any of the people in this history is of Lucy Ricketts standing outside the Farmhouse in her widow's weeds. She has the one-piece black bombazine bosom of the Victorian era and looks ferocious. Later evidence suggests she was a bit of a martinet. Walter's will is the first not to describe his wife as his dear or beloved wife and although Lucy has a fine gravestone Walter is not included on it, or elsewhere in the Great Comberton churchyard.

Walter mortgaged the farm with a loan from Lucy's brother Joseph for £450 on the 14th January 1873. Although the mortgage was transferred a number of times, it was only paid off by Annie Munslow on the 8th December 1937, long after Joseph's death.[94] The period from 1870's to 1900 was a difficult time for farmers, sometimes referred to as the Great Depression of British Agriculture, caused by the dramatic fall in grain prices following the opening up of the American prairies to cultivation in the 1870s and the advent of cheap transportation with the rise of steamships – 1882 saw the first arrival of refrigerated New Zealand lamb. In addition, in 1883 Krakatoa ejected over 20 cubic kilometres of rock into the atmosphere in the form of ash which travelled around the world, with significant adverse climatic effects. In the circumstances Walter can perhaps be forgiven for retaining the loan.

Littlebury's Directory of 1879 gives us a picture of farming in Great Comberton in that year recording crops grown as wheat, barley, beans, turnips and mangold with extensive growth of fruit and a choice sort of cider.

Walter died on 12th December 1875 aged 50 and his will, the shortest in this history and dated 23rd May 1864 reads:

This is the last Will and Testament of me Walter Ricketts of Great Comberton in the County of Worcester Yeoman. I give devise and bequeath unto my Wife Lucy Ricketts for her own use absolutely All my real and personal estate whatsoever and wheresoever And all property over which I have a disposing power, subject only to the payment of my just debts funeral and testamentary expenses and I appoint her sole Executrix ….

13 Lucy Ricketts 1831 - 1922

By 1881 Walter had died and Lucy was described in the census as a farmer of 14 acres employing one man. She outlived Walter by 47 years surviving to 91. She never married again, but was evidently active in village affairs, for example in 1894 she was serving as an Overseer of the Poor. She had two visitors on the 1881 census day, Jane Carmell, a spinster of 23 born in Cropthorne, and William J Gibbs, a batchelor of 20 born in Hanbury. Pool House was rented out to William Groves, listed in Bentley's directory of 1840 as a carpenter. Lucy's sister Ann Hardy was living in Vine Cottage in Russell Street with her son Alfred Henry Hardy. In 1891 Lucy was no longer living alone. She had a domestic servant and groom, Charles Mince aged 17 from Birlingham, and her niece (as recorded by the census enumerator but actually her great-niece) Annie Hardy had come to live with her. In 1901 Lucy and Annie were still living in the Farmhouse and Alfred H. Hardy, her 40-year-old nephew had come to live in the cottage and work on the farm, after the death of his mother Ann in 1894. She also had a cattleman, George Bateman, aged 15 and born in Birlingham. On 29th September 1905 Lucy bought Lammas Meadow and Penns Orchard[95] from John Whoods George of 236

---

94   BA12083 899.1208
95   These are the two fields bordering the road to Little Comberton north of Lower End Farm

Bridge Street, Port Melbourne in the Colony of Victoria Australia for £540 bringing the holding up to 24 acres. John Whoods was allocated these two fields in 1820 at Inclosure and left them, along with his other land and house, now Orchard Cottage next to Kent's Farm, to his wife Ann for her lifetime and then to his daughter Ann wife of Edmund George. Ann George died on the 6th December 1904, and John Whoods George, her eldest son and heir sold the land, although he saw none of the money, for the estate was subject to three mortgages totalling £900.

The name Lammas Meadow was applied to a particular type of medieval land tenure. Under this management regime, the owner, traditionally the Lord of the Manor in which the meadow lay, divided the meadow into parcels of land referred to as lots or doles. He then sold the rights to the hay crop to local farmers who were responsible for harvesting the hay in each allotment. However, after the hay crop has been gathered, the meadow became common pasture and the livestock of certain commoners were entitled to graze the entire meadow regardless of the hay rights. Traditionally, the commonable rights began on August 12th, also known as Lammas day, and ended around Candlemas at the beginning of February when once again the meadow was laid up for hay. As far as is known, this system of land management had survived relatively unchanged for the past 800 years. Lammas is a medieval English name derived from the Anglo-Saxon *hlaef-mass* or 'loaf mass' festival held on August 1st to mark the opening of the harvest. The first of the ripe cereals were picked, baked into bread, consecrated at church and on the 12th, they were crumbled into the four corners of a barn to make it a safe repository for the grain about to arrive there. This festival appears in the Anglo-Saxon Chronicle of 912 as 'the feast of the first fruits'. Cricklade North Meadow is a famous example of an undamaged Lammas Meadow.

Lammas Meadow in Great Comberton had been sold off and ceased to be common before 1676 when it was sold by Bridgett Lampitt of Broadway to Thomas Clarke of Great Comberton.[96]

By 1911 Lucy was 79 and Annie's father John, Alfred Henry's brother, had come to Great Comberton. John is listed as having 8 children, seven living and was a gardener on his own account at home. Lucy is still given as the farmer of land which was all pasture and orchards with Alfred Henry to help on the farm, and Annie helping in dairy work, and there was also a servant / cowman, William Fisher, aged 17 born in Besford. Alfred Henry Hardy had died before the next census date and was buried here, his gravestone reads:

In Memory of Alfred Henry Hardy died Febry 18th 1921 Aged 61 years. Rest in Peace

---

96   BA 351 705.81 18

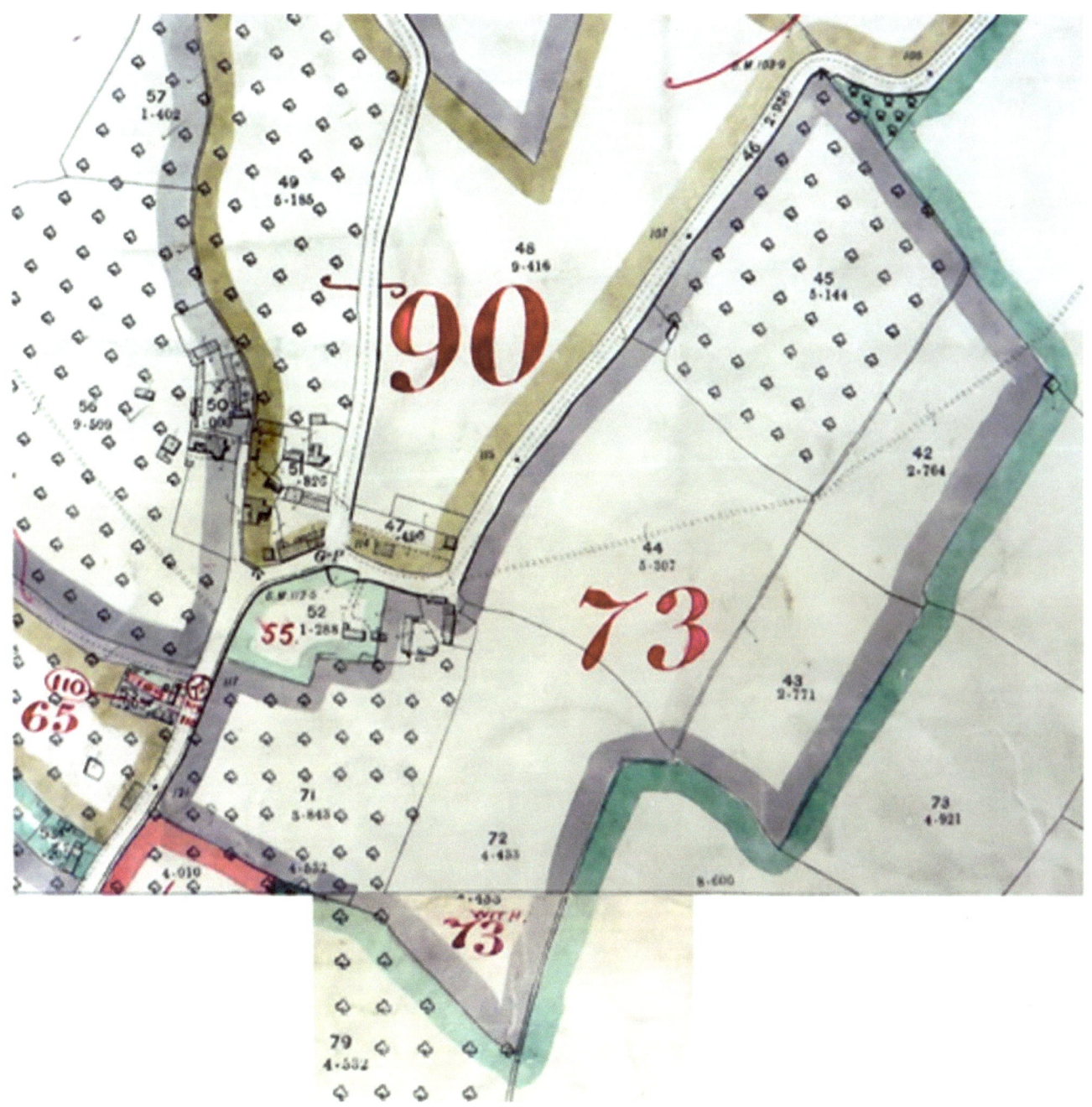

Lower End Farm on the 1809 Plan of the Parish of Great Comberton.

The 1909-10 Inland Revenue Land Valuation (map shown above) and the 1911 census show that Pool House was rented out to Allan Heeks, who was a jobbing gardener, with his wife Eliza and four children and the Bothy at Lower End Farm was *derelict and used as a storehouse*. It also notes the sale price of Lammas Meadow and Penns Orchard as *cheap*.[97] Lucy Ricketts died on the 5th November 1922, and in her will she left the Farmhouse, the cottage and barn with 13 acres to Annie Hardy and John Hardy as joint tenants. Pool House and the two fields Lucy added to the farm in 1905 were left to Annie absolutely. Annie also owned Vine Cottage which Lucy sold her for £180 in 1909 when it was described as:

All that messuage or tenement with the gardens, outbuildings, hereditaments, premises and appurtenances thereto belonging situate in Great Comberton aforesaid, for many years in the occupation of Joseph Smith,

---
97 BA 8585/1/14

afterwards of Jane Smith (Lucy's brother and sister) *and since of the Reverend Nathanial Shelmerdine or his undertenant and now void.*[98]

The wording on Lucy's grave is the only suggestion that she may have had a kinder side, or perhaps she was more lovable in retrospect. It reads:

In loving memory of Lucy, wife of Walter Ricketts who died Novr 5th 1922 aged 91 years. There remaineth a rest to the people of God.

Lucy Ricketts outside Lower End Farm possibly around 1890.

98 Vine Cottage private deeds

HARDY

Lower End Farm

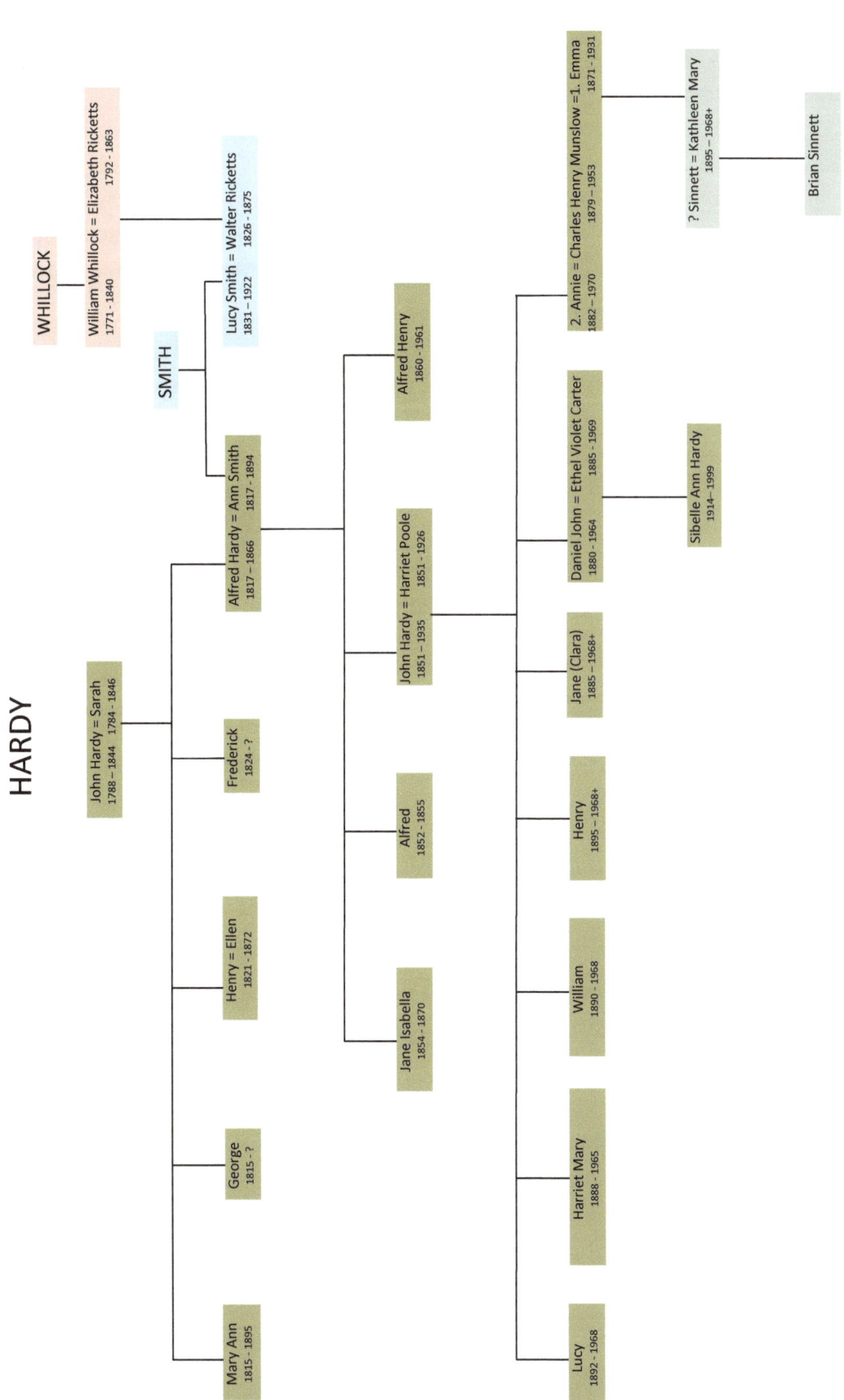

14 John Hardy 1851 – 1935 and his children

John Hardy was born at Croome on 25th June 1851, one of four children of Alfred Hardy and Lucy Ricketts' sister Ann, two of the daughters of Edmund Smith V of Vine Cottage. In order, they were Jane Isabella, baptised 29th October 1854, Alfred baptised 23rd November 1852 and buried 28th July 1855, John, baptised 25th June 1851, and Alfred Henry baptised 25th March 1860. Alfred was a kitchen gardener at Croome; the 1861 census has him living in the kitchen gardens with his wife and three children and a nursemaid, and Billings' Directory of 1855 lists him as Gardener to the Earl of Coventry. Alfred's father John was also a gardener at Croome, and since he too was born there his grandfather may have worked at Croome as well. Alfred's brother Henry Hardy was the landlord of the Coventry Arms in High Green, Croome a licence carried on by his wife after his death in 1872.

Henry succeeded Joseph Lane and his wife Mary at the Coventry Arms, a fine five-bay double-pile red-brick building which still stands next to the estate office although it is no longer a pub. Mary Lane, née Mary Ricketts, and her sister Ann were the daughters of Matthew Ricketts, farmer of Woollas and brother of Elizabeth Whillock. Elizabeth Whillock's daughter-in-law Lucy Smith was the sister of Ann Smith who was Henry Hardy's sister-in-law. This little web of relationships perfectly illustrates the multiple interconnections between all the families in this history.

In 1871 his sister-in-law, Alfred's widow Ann and her son Alfred Henry were living at the Coventry Arms with Henry, and must have moved to Great Comberton after he died. Alfred and Ann, Henry and their sister Mary Ann are all buried at Croome.

John went as an under-gardener to Trentham in Staffordshire where he was recorded in the 1871 census living in a bothy with 9 other gardeners. He had left Trentham and was in Great Comberton on 6th December 1876 when he placed an advertisement in the Manchester Courier and Lancashire General Advertiser for work:

Gardener, Head, age 25, single; thoroughly practical in all branches of the profession; first-class recommendations – JH Great Comberton near Pershore, Worcestershire.

He evidently didn't find work in Lancashire for in 1878 he was at Berkeley in Gloucestershire where he met and married Harriet Poole on 3rd December. By 1881 he was a gardener and domestic servant in Milverton near Leamington Spa, and from there he went to Newmarket before 1891, also as a gardener and domestic servant, where he remained until he came back to Great Comberton before 1911.

John and Harriet had seven children: Daniel John born 12 January 1880, Annie born 1st January 1882, Clara Jane born 13th August 1885, Harriet Mary born 1888, William born 1890, Lucy born 1892 and Henry born 1895. It was often the case that large families would share their children with childless relatives, particularly where they were rich childless relatives, and so Annie was sent to live with her great aunt Lucy Ricketts. A postcard dated September 30th 1904 from Annie to her sister Clara Jane gives an insight into her life:

Please be sure & not send me anything at all dear, as Aunt Lucy is so cross at you wanting to send a B.P. keep it and save up all you can for yourself never mind me just now, much love from Nancy.[99]

What a B.P. might have been is anyone's guess. John Hardy's granddaughter remembers being told that Lucy was bedridden towards the end of her life and would bang on the floor with her cane when she wanted anything.

---

[99] Salisbury family private documents

John Hardy died on the 8th January 1935 leaving his half of Lower End Farm to his son Daniel John. He and Harriet are buried in Pirton.

15 Annie Hardy 1882 – 1970

Annie Hardy lived at Lower End Farm from before 1891 when the census recorded her as 8 years old, and attended the village school in what is now the Village Hall. Mrs Shelmerdine, the rector's wife, recorded her attendance at a school treat on 5th August 1896 in her diary.[100] She helped Lucy Ricketts about the farm and in the dairy and, on 20th June 1903, she entered her butter in a special class in the Herefordshire and Worcestershire Agricultural Society Show in Worcester open to pupils who had received instruction under the Worcestershire County Council and was highly commended, the judges commenting that *the work throughout was exceedingly good and there was much difficulty in adjudicating the prizes.*[101]

Annie's family visited fairly often. Pershore station opened in 1852 so it would not have been difficult to get to Great Comberton from Newmarket. She was close to her sisters and they exchanged postcards which are collected in an album owned by the Salisbury family. Her sister Clara Jane worked at the Villa Signorina, Fordham Road, Newmarket, owned by Signore Eduardo Ginistrelli. Ginistrelli came to Newmarket in 1887 from Italy, and he had moderate success with his mare Signorina after which he named his stud. Signorina and a teaser stallion of little value would call to each other and Ginistrelli decided they were in love and, against the advice and in the face of mockery from all his racing friends, decided to breed from them. The result was a filly called Signorinetta.

Signoretta.

He was vindicated when in 1908, ridden by Billy Bullock, she won the Derby at 100:1 followed by the Oaks two days later. Two years later Ginistrelli married and built Oaks Lodge which still stands, although

---
100   Great Comberton scrapbooks
101   Worcestershire Chronicle, Saturday 20th June 1903

his stud farm has vanished under the Oaks Business Park. He sold Signorinetta to Lord Rosebery for 10,000 guineas and the horse never won another race.[102]

Annie's brother William farmed at Knight's Villa, Pirton, not far from Croome, and Henry, Lucy, Harriet Mary and Clara Jane also lived there along with Anne Poole, probably their mother's sister. John Hardy may also have gone to live in Pirton since he was buried there when he died in 1935.

Annie Hardy married Charles Munslow. Brian Sinnett, Charles's grandson by his first wife, recalled Charles and Annie in an email, the latter as *a very kind person who I remember with great affection*:

They lived in Eckington in a distinctive bungalow opposite the vicarage, which my grandfather designed and built for her in a South African colonial style. The bungalow, now much altered, has now sadly lost its distinctive veranda which made it quite unusual. My memory is that this was in fact the second house, which he built for her in Eckington. We called Annie Auntie Nann as children and I imagine my grandfather Charles must have died when I was about seven or eight. He gave me my first riding lesson in a style that for many years I was never to encounter again. This colonial riding style, I was to find out many years later, was apparently the way the British army taught their raw recruits how to ride very quickly. Charlie was part of a voluntary expeditionary force, which was raised in Worcester and he was one of only three men who survived to train a secondary force, which arrived some years later. My grandfather was an excellent horseman long before he went to the Boer War; my mother told me that he had ridden a black Mustang horse when in Africa which tellingly he gave the name of Satan. This horse, along with many others, I was to find many years later had apparently been a gift from the American Government to help the British in this war, which they were at the time rapidly losing. My grandfather was of course a new sort of soldier, which this war seems to have invented as a mounted terrorist and Charles job was specifically to terrorise the Boer farmers families off their land, to stop them re supplying their men. I am somewhat embarrassed to say that there is little doubt that he greatly enjoyed the excitement of being a mounted terrorist, which at this time seems to have been a respected new form of modern warfare. It was certainly this sort of activity, which eventually paid off for the British, to win this war. It is likely that this riding style was part of what the Americans gave to the British, along with several boatloads of Mustang horses. It is also possible that they probably even gave the British the notion of terrorism, which when the buffalo were all shot, the Seventh Cavalry found it easy to put an end to "the Indian Problem". Interestingly he taught me that you should ride like you walk or march and it was basically this colonial riding style, which I still teach today, as western riding.

As a child I spent so many hours reading the Womans Own magazine while smelling the foul smell of geraniums in Annie's front room. So I am not likely to forget the experience that this form of persecution held for me. My mother Kathleen had become very fond of her step mother and she regularly took me and my sister to visit her all the way from Cheltenham, for more years than I care to remember. I should think than Nan (Annie) died just before I got married in 1968 and I well remember my mother urging me to go and visit Annie with my future wife Carolyn to ask her if she might leave me some farm land that she owned in her will. This must be your farm today and needless to say she sadly did not leave it to me, all I really know is that it was arable land which was very close to the river. This may be of help to you because her story was that it had been in the ownership of her family for many generations and she believed it must stay in the ownership of the blood of her family, which I strangely seem to remember were the Ricketts, although through marriage I assume they were then probably called Hardy. Sibelle was the joint executor of my step grandmother Annie's

---

[102] http://www.newmarketlhs.org.uk/oakspark.htm

will, with my mother Kathleen and the only thing I can remember about Sibelle was that to my mothers extreme annoyance, it was that she had hardly ever bothered to visit Annie and she inherited nearly everything. When Annie was dying, my mother brought her back to Cheltenham where she stayed with us for a short time but she soon became so frail that she went into a nursing home where she quickly passed away. I remember that Annie also owned a row of tenanted cottages in Berkeley which, on her death, she left to the tenants. My grandfather became a market gardener and green grocer after the Boer War, he had apparently lied about his age to enlist but when the first world war started he was too old at thirty but he immediately once again volunteered for service. He wound up being bayonetted seven times in a trench in Bulgaria, where he spent two years in a prisoner of war camp and then walked all the way back to Worcester when the war had ended. He had then been officially presumed killed and lost in action for three years but had miraculously turned up with little memory, sitting at the kitchen table when my mother and her sister had come home from school. Charles first wife Emma, my real grandmother, then sadly lost her tenanted shop in Worcester mainly because Charlie had refused to help her purchase the shop, which had been offered to them at a very reduced cost. The shop had been owned by the Worcester Perrins sauce family, my grandfather took the irrational point of view that as a war veteran, he should be exempt from being forced to purchase any shop. In truth, Charles was mentally burnt out and very resentful that after all his military service he had no war pension. The family were eventually thrown out onto the street but the British Legion soon found them a cottage in Perton where my grandmother Emma soon sadly died of a heart condition. The family then eventually moved back to Worcester and it was here that Charles met Annie when going to church. Charles soon married Annie, and my mother who had met my father in Perton, also soon married. My mother and father moved to Cheltenham in 1938 to a tenanted farm which happily I was able to purchase some twenty six years ago now. One thing that I remember was that my step grandmother Annie had a sister who strangely dressed exactly like a man. She wore a flat cap and boots and to all purposes dressed completely like a man, my mother did her best to explain that she was apparently a rural transvestite who lived with a friend in a cottage at Comberton. I think her name was Pip but I am not really sure about that because I only met her once, she was however quite a talking point for a child to behold.[103]

On the 16th December 1937 Daniel John bought Annie Hardy out of her half share of Lower End Farm for £450, with the help of a mortgage for £150 from his brother William in Pirton which he paid off in 1947, although Annie saw none of the proceeds since they paid off Walter Ricketts' mortgage of 64 years previously. This is the first document to give a name to the farm. Annie retained Lammas Meadow and Penns Orchard, which she left to Sibelle Hardy, along with Pool House, in her will, once again bringing the holding back to 24 acres. The land was valued at £1250 and Pool House at £500. She sold Vine Cottage to John Reginald Peart and Mrs M Peart in 1936. Interestingly the conveyance records the property immediately to the west as being owned by Daniel Hardy.[104]

The 1941-1943 Farm Survey map, reproduced below, shows the farm as it was then, Penn's Orchard and the field behind Pool House are still orchards, as is the area now occupied by Hands Orchard and the field behind Tibbitts Farm.

---

103 Brian Sinnett pers com 27th September 2010
104 Vine Cottage private deeds

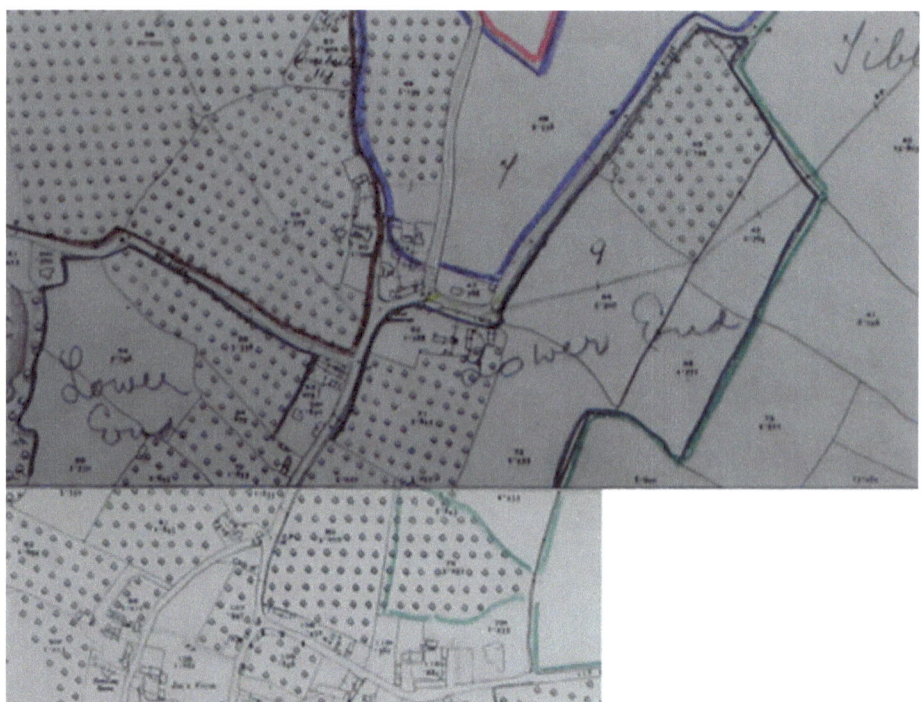

Lower End Farm on the 1941-1943 Farm Survey map.

Annie Munslow née Hardy died on the 6th May 1970 aged 88 and is buried in Pirton along with Charles and his first wife Emma.

16 Daniel John Hardy 1880 – 1964

Daniel John was born in Berkeley while his father was still working there, and was always known as John Hardy, in Great Comberton at least. He was living with his parents in Newmarket in 1891, and in 1911 he was a servant living with three other servants above stables at Moulton Paddocks outside Newmarket. He married Ethel Violet Carter later in 1911 in Epping, and their only child Sibelle Ann was born in Buckhurst, Essex in 1914.

John and Annie Hardy handed over their stock to Daniel John after a valuation on 27th March 1926 which listed:

Tommy, brown pony. 3 calves, 2 roan dairy cows, 4 yearlings, 2 cows due, 30 fowls.

A 4 ½ inch cart, sprung market cart, light spring dray, dog cart, harness, troughs, tools, milk and cream kit, 4 hogsheads 1924 cider 5 do 1925, 2 empty.

In Grain (?) Field – portable fowl house. In Pasture Field – tump of hay, wheat straw valued at £281.15.6

Paid 18th December 1933 less £62 for four yearlings received by Miss A Hardy.[105]

This transfer to Daniel John is confirmed in the agricultural return for 4th June 1941: it was addressed to Mr D J Hardy and he indicated that he had occupied the holding for the past 16 years.[106] Although he had no arable land, there were 9 acres of orchards (unchanged from 1910) and the 15 acres of permanent grass was split between 5 for grazing and 10 for mowing. He did not employ any labour and he had no horses or tractor on the holding at this date: his livestock comprised 2 cows in milk, 4 other cattle and 120 poultry.

---

105   Salisbury family private documents
106   TNA: MAF32/63/111

The National Farm Survey was undertaken at the farm on 2nd July 1941 and the following points are of note from the survey:

- Mr D J Hardy was the owner of Lower End Farm and he was a full-time farmer who did not occupy any other land;
- The soil was described as 100% medium and the farm was conveniently laid out;
- Access to both roads and railway was good;
- The condition of the farmhouse and buildings was good: there were no cottages associated with the farm and no farm roads;
- Fences were good, but the ditches and field drainage were only fair;
- There were no infestations of pests or weeds and no derelict fields;
- Water supply to the farmhouse was from a well: there was no supply to the farm buildings and the fields were watered from the well or from streams – there was no seasonal shortage of water;
- There was a public electricity supply used for both lighting and power, but only for household purposes;
- The condition of the arable and pasture land was described as fair, with fertilisers being used to some extent on both;
- The farm was classified as B, due to a lack of capital.

Therefore he was farming in Great Comberton from 1925, before he inherited his father's half share of the farm in 1935, and he consolidated his holding with the purchase of the other half from Annie Munslow in 1937, although she still retained Lammas Meadow and Penns Orchard which must be the land Brian Sinnett hoped to inherit. He borrowed £150 from his brother William Hardy on the 25th December 1937, presumably to fund the purchase, and paid it back on the 3rd June 1947.

If he was cutting 10 acres of mowing grass in 1941 with no horses or tractor he was seriously behind the times, as mechanical assistance was in use from the 1850's. Without additional labour the task would have been virtually impossible so we have to assume he contracted at least part of the work out. Although he said he had no arable land, in 1926 he had acquired wheat straw, so may have converted some of the arable land to orchards in the meantime. Also he must have been farming Lammas Meadow and Penns Orchard which were still owned by Annie Munslow. On the other hand, it was stated that there were no cottages associated with the farm when we know the Bothy was there, so we cannot discount a tenuous relationship with the actual state of affairs in the return.

The electricity supply was the subject of an easement granted to the Shropshire, Worcestershire and Staffordshire Electric Power Company on the 8th May 1939 for an annual rent of 3s.

Daniel John Hardy died of heart failure aged 50 on the 27th June 1964 and is buried in Great Comberton churchyard. His grave reads:

In loving memory of Daniel John Hardy born January 12th 1880 died June 27th 1964 and Ethel Violet Hardy born June 5th 1885 died July 19th 1969

Since he left no will, his wife Ethel Violet was granted Letters of Administration over his estate and she immediately passed Lower End Farm on to Sibelle who was living with her parents in Great Comberton, saying in her Deed of Gift, dated the 2nd December 1964:

In consideration of her natural love and affection for the Donee the Donor hereby conveys unto the Donee ALL THAT messuage or tenement and farm buildings situate in the Parish of Great Comberton in the County of Worcester and ALL THOSE three pieces or parcels of pasture land and orcharding situate and adjoining the property first hereinbefore described consisting of a meadow and orchard and a field called "The Piece" or "The Ley" containing together Thirteen acres and Two roods or thereabout TO HOLD the same unto the Donee in fee simple.

The deed was witnessed by Fred Wallace Manton.

Lower End Farm and Pool House early 1960's.

17 Sibelle Hardy 1914 – 1999

Sibelle was a shy and reserved character. She never married but was engaged for most of her adult life to Fred Manton, a builder who lived in Knight's Buildings in Pershore. Fred's sister Joy married Reg Salisbury. Elsie Heeks remained living in Pool House after her father Allan's death in 1951, and after she died, Sibelle gave Pool house to Reg and Joy. They moved to Great Comberton about 1981 with their daughter Lyn, and were effectively the family Sibelle never had. Reg said that Sibelle and Fred never married because Sibelle thought they weren't compatible, despite having been engaged for over 50 years. After the death of Sibelle's parents, Fred came to Lower End Farm to live with her.

Most of the period features of the Farmhouse were lost in Fred's improvements over the years. Plain clay roof tiles were replaced with concrete, and the slates off the barns with corrugated asbestos-cement sheet. The Farmhouse was roughcast rendered, the old windows were replaced with Crittal type metal frames, and the old panelled doors with flush doors. One of the two huge back-to-back inglenooks was filled in with an elaborate, and much more efficient, brickette fireplace. The two wings at the north and south ends remained untouched, and virtually derelict. At the same time he did, for the first time, provide the house with an inside toilet and a bathroom.

After Annie Munslow died, Sibelle appropriated Lammas Meadow and Penns Orchard as part of her share of Annie's estate which was split between her, Henry and Clara Jane Hardy after various bequests. They were valued at £1250. None of Sibelle's siblings had any children, and gradually she inherited their estates.

On 14th April 1975 Sibelle granted an easement to the British Gas Corporation for a consideration of £130 0s 38d allowing them to run a distribution main across Town Furlong on the length between Mongcroft Road and the governor station opposite Pool House.

As she got older Sibelle became more withdrawn, and was burgled twice, the second time thieves made off with an entire safe and its contents. Eventually she moved into Bricklehampton Hall and Lower End Farm remained empty for a number of years until finally she asked Reg Salisbury to sell it on her behalf. The cider mill in the barn, the lias floor slabs in the cottage and various other features such as pumps, troughs and cooking ranges were also sold. Twenty acres were tenanted by Gerry Hickey, who had married the daughter of a local farmer, and four acres by Hugh Peart, whose family went back several generations in the village. Neither had a formal tenancy agreement of any kind and where Hugh agreed to quit, Gerry claimed a protected tenancy, hoping to buy the land at a reduced price.

Sibelle Hardy died on 9th April 1999.

COLLINGWOOD

18 Kate Collingwood

I bought Lower End Farm at auction at the Angel Hotel on Thursday 11th December 1997. Hugh Peart gave up his tenancy on the 4 acres of the land he had been farming in 1999 but remained growing broad beans by consent on a small part of it until 2018 when he retired fully. Gerry Hickey was greatly annoyed to be outbid for the 20 acres, remaining a tenant until late 2002 when it became uneconomic and he quit. Lammas Meadow had been ploughed and turned over to arable sometime after 1941, when the Agricultural Return recorded 10 acres of grass for mowing, 5 acres of grass for grazing and 9 acres of orchard with grass beneath. The pasture and ridge and furrow in Town Furlong survived until the 1960s. With the help of the Countryside Stewardship Scheme I restored it all to permanent pasture and meadow, replanting hedges and a small wood, and reinstating the orchard with traditional fruit trees.

The Farm was virtually derelict when I bought it. The Bothy was covered in ivy, daylight was visible through the roof and the upstairs floor was unsafe. The barn was a shell, with a lean to where the kitchen is now. The Farmhouse itself was barely habitable, but the brickette fireplace worked and there was an immersion heater for hot water, so I moved in before Christmas. The conversion of the barn and the extensions and refurbishments to the Farmhouse and Bothy were designed for me by Walter Thomson of Associated Architects and constructed by P Williams and Son of Defford.

Lower End Farm 1997.

TIMELINE

Before Inclosure parishes such as Great Comberton were farmed collectively in a system which probably dates back to the 8th or 9th century, whereby a number of large open fields, five in Great Comberton before Inclosure in 1820, were divided into strips or sellions which we still see as ridge and furrow in fields that have not been ploughed since 1820. This characteristic feature of the open field systems of midland landscapes results from the use of a plough team of six oxen and a heavy mouldboard plough throwing the soil inwards to the high point of the ridges. Individual owners and tenants would be allocated ridges sprinkled around in various different fields; a typical holding would be about 20 acres in total, but the fields would be worked communally. The whole of one field would be set down to a single crop, rotating between the five fields, being typically wheat, barley, beans and fallow. Around the end of the eighteenth century there was a general movement to do away with the open fields as inefficient, and this was carried out by way of agreement or by Parliamentary Act. In the case of Great Comberton the Inclosure Act of 1820 explains the motivation:

Whereas there are within the Parish of Great Comberton in the County of Worcester, divers open and common fields, meadows pastures and commonable lands and waste grounds …. Intermingled and dispersed and are inconveniently situated for the owners thereof.

Thomas Fulljames of Hasfield Court in the County of Gloucester was appointed sole Commissioner with the responsibility to allocate land fairly. Major landowners such as the Hanfords of Woollas Hall, Lords of the Manor in Great Comberton, were concerned to demonstrate their rights, and Charles Hanford commissioned Thomas Collingridge, his sometime agent, surveyor and gamekeeper, to map his holdings in the Parish in 1809. The combination of this map and the 1820 Inclosure Award plan allow us to see exactly how the Parish landholdings changed in the process.

The four most northerly fields of Lower End Farm, Lammas Meadow, Penns Orchard and the Upper and Lower Ley were historically meadow. The remaining fields were all part of Town Furlong which extended right across to Russell Street and was part of Churchill Field. The traces of ridge and furrow ploughed flat are still visible in Town Furlong; not by changes in level but by differences in the sward, particularly dandelions. These traces show that the ridge and furrow which survives in the orchard north of Tibbitts Farm would have extended into the Lower End Farm part of Town Furlong. By reputation Lammas Meadow had been a species-rich hay meadow and is regaining some of this diversity although it will be many years before it fully recovers from the effects of nitrogen fertiliser. In 2024 it, and Penns Orchard, the two traditionally managed hay fields, were designated a Local Wildlife Site by Worcestershire Wildlife Trust.

In 2024 three ponds and a flood attenuation pond were excavated in the Upper and Lower Leys on the east side of the farm. These two fields were also part of the village meadows but have always lain wet in parts. The Horsley Ditch, which flows off Bredon Hill rises very rapidly in heavy rain and the flood attenuation pond will catch this flood and release it slowly through a leaky dam, slowing its progress to the Avon. In the course of excavation both clay and plastic land drains were uncovered, the former may have come from a brickworks in Kempsey by river. Machine-made clay land drains became cheap enough for mass use after

1852, and there would have been an incentive for landowners to drain land after Inclosure in 1820.

Dutch elm disease ravaged this landscape. Elm suckers in hedges and massive elm stumps together with trees shown on old maps indicate that hedgerows were once much richer in trees. Now we face the loss of almost all the ash to ash dieback. It is interesting to note the frequency of hops in the eastern boundary of the fields where the area beyond was called Hopyard in 1820. Penns Orchard and the field behind Pool House were both shown as orchard on the 1st edition Ordnance Survey map of 1885. Penns was still shown as orchard on the 1970 edition but the field behind Pool House showed no trees although a few old plums and damsons survived in 1997.

In 2005 I planted five acorns harvested from the best oak tree in the parish which grows beside the footpath to Nafford. The parent tree is about 350 years old and it would therefore have germinated in Thomas Wright's lifetime and has outlived everyone who ever owned Lower End Farm in the past.

Nothing in the records tells us which part of Lower End Farm was built by Sibill Wright with the £8 left to her by her husband.

1809 map by Thomas Collingridge.

The first map showing the layout of Lower End Farm is the 1809 Thomas Collingridge plan of the parish which shows the Farmhouse as a short building and the barn in two sections. The normal convention with maps is that north is towards the top of the map. Thomas Collingridge drew this map looking towards Bredon Hill so with south to the top, probably reflecting the way most of us perceive the landscape here.

An undated plan of the village shows the occupiers of each house. The Farmhouse was occupied by George Whillock and the Bothy and barn by Mrs Whillock which puts the date of the map between 1814 and 1819. Again the map faces towards Bredon Hill, although here it has been rotated to make the text more readable.

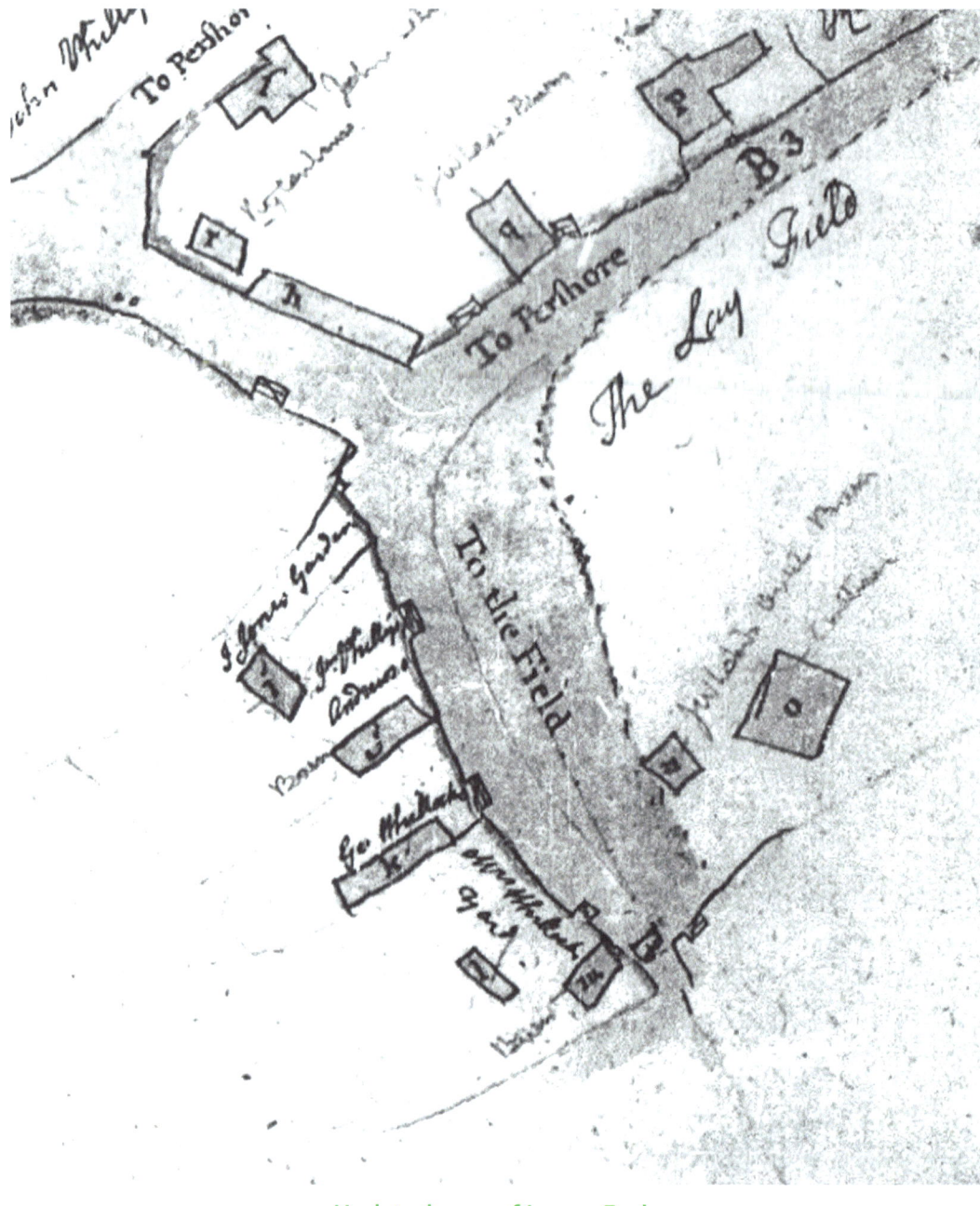

Undated map of Lower End.

The Farmhouse is shown as a long building, extending well beyond the back of the Bothy, and the barn is shown much shorter and close up to the road.

Although these two maps give a general indication of the disposition of buildings neither is intended as a survey, the purpose of the first being to establish the landholdings of the Hanfords before Inclosure, and the second to identify occupiers, and we cannot therefore place too much reliance on them in detail. On the other hand it is likely that most of the extensions to the Farmhouse happened after George Whillock bought it from Charles Cross in 1818.

The 1820 Inclosure Award plan is perhaps a more reliable indication of the layout of the buildings. It shows the Farmhouse little larger than the Bothy, which is in about its present position relative to the barn. A second barn is shown behind the main barn. The cowshed along the road frontage has not yet been built. The barn on the road frontage between Pool House and the Farmhouse is no longer there.

1820 Inclosure Award plan.

By the time of the first OS map in 1885 the buildings are roughly in the shape they retained in 1997, the cowshed is there and the barn has wings to the north and south.

1885 Ordnance Survey map.

The Farmhouse is built of soft red hand-made bricks, with some integrated random pieces of timber. It has clearly been substantially altered over its life and it is therefore not easy to sequence the changes. The roof of the central section has very substantial oak king-post trusses with tenoned and pegged joints but the purlins have been altered; the upper ones are aligned with the trusses and rafters but the lower ones are butted between the trusses and set in the vertical plane which requires each rafter to be birdsmouthed over it. The inference from this is that the roof was originally built by someone who knew what they were doing but subsequently altered in a very amateur fashion.

The north wing, which contained the kitchen and a dairy down three steps from the kitchen in 1997, was built in two stages so that the dairy was an extension to the kitchen which was itself an extension to the central block. Similarly the southern wing is an extension although there may have been a single story wing before it was enlarged as the straight joint does not extend to the ground. Neither wing continues the dentil course at the eaves found on the central block. In 1997 there was a lias slab floor, much damaged, in the south wing which is retained and a blue-brick floor laid on earth in the dairy; all the other ground floors had been replaced with concrete. The two large inglenook fireplaces back to back were probably built at different times as the chimneys do not match although they are joined where the emerge from the roof.

An old photograph of Lucy Ricketts dating from around 1890 shows what was then the front of the house facing west: the back was facing the farmyard at that date. It has brick walls in Flemish garden wall bond.

The windows have square-topped brick arches over on the ground floor and timber lintels upstairs with six-pane wrought-iron casements of which the bottom two panes on one side form an opening light. The roof is of cambered plain clay tiles with a dentil course below. There is also a porch formed of a curved metal hood on wrought iron supports, which was rescued by Hugh Peart and returned for replacement. The front is mostly covered in vegetation including what looks like an espaliered pear and a wisteria. Part of both wings is visible.

By 1997 the plain clay roof tiles had been replaced by concrete, possibly this is when the roof structure was altered. The old windows had been removed and replaced by Crittal type metal frames and the outside rendered. The staircase was not in its original position since one of the main cross beams had been cut to accommodate it; most of the original doors had gone, replaced by modern flush doors, apart from one three-plank door upstairs and one Georgian door downstairs. One of the two large fireplaces which lie back to back in the centre of the house had been infilled with an ornate brickette fireplace. Most of this work must have been carried out by Fred Manton, Sibelle Hardy's fiancé.

Thomas Smith may have lived in the Farmhouse until he went to Tewkesbury. He was in Great Comberton in 1746 and Tewkesbury when he wrote his will in 1773, and probably much earlier since his daughter Elizabeth married John Wakefield in Tewkesbury in 1762. It is unlikely that Elizabeth Wakefield ever lived here as her husband was an established bargemaster of Gloucester, and her niece Elizabeth and Charles Cross married in Birmingham and lived in Tibberton so they were probably absentee landlords too. We therefore don't know who was occupying the Farmhouse from about 1750 to 1798 when the Land Tax returns tell us that George Whillock occupied it before he bought it. It may be that Thomas and Susannah Whillock lived there after they married in 1759 and Susannah handed the lease over to George after she was widowed in 1788. Thomas Smith's sister-in-law Hannah Wright was Susannah's brother-in law Thomas Wright's first cousin so there is a remote link. An old board which was reused in a small enclosure in the barn has the letters HMP and HMT crudely carved into it along with either EP or ED and 1747 and two Ws. It does not shed any further light on the question sadly, particularly since virtually every family associated with Lower End has the initial W.

We can be more certain of the date of the stone wall from the Farmhouse out to the entrance to the yard. During rebuilding in 2020 this was found to contain large quantities of smelting slag which strongly points to Thomas or George Whillock as its builder.

The Bothy has a timber frame between the two downstairs rooms, and the stone part of the chimney gave way to brick higher up with an irregular boundary between the two. The chimney extended to the north side into a ruined construction which may have either formed part of the forge or have been an open wash house.

The roof had been raised at some stage, reusing the original purlins which are much less substantial than those in the Farmhouse, so this was originally a ground floor with storage only above. It also had a lias slab floor which was sold before 1997, along with pumps and troughs in the farmyard.

The original bricks on the front face of the Bothy are 63 x 220mm. They are high quality hand-made facing bricks and at some time the joints have had a lime putty applied, normally done to make the joints appear finer and thus the construction of higher status.

Parliament fixed brick sizes in 1776 at 8.5 x 4 x 2.5 inches (216 x 102 x 63mm). Fighting wars is expensive, and in 1784, after the American War of Independence, parliament taxed each brick used, so some bricks were made larger, up to 10 x 5 x 3ins (254 x 127 x 76mm). In 1803, these large bricks were further taxed, and this was avoided by reducing the size to 9 x 4.5 x 3ins (229 x 114 x 76mm). In 1850 the brick taxes were repealed, and brick sizes gradually standardised, rising four courses per foot (304mm), except in the north of England where they rose four courses per 13 inches (330mm) for much of the nineteenth century.[107]

If the Bothy was the house Sibill Wright built for £8 it was probably only two rooms with a timber frame which was later refaced in brick and subsequently extended upwards to give sufficient headroom for two further rooms on the first floor. The size of the bricks suggests the brickwork predates 1784.

Bricks from the barn and cowshed.

The cowshed is not on the 1820 Inclosure Award plan but is shown on the 1885 Ordnance Survey map. Given that the barn uses the same bricks as the cowshed it is likely that it was rebuilt when the cowshed was constructed. The bricks are machine made, of a type found in various places in the village, with two square holes lengthways. These bricks cannot therefore be used for the headers in bonded brickwork so a second type with 20 smaller holes in the bed is also made.

This is an illogical design, so there must have been an advantage to the two-hole version which made it worthwhile, and this is probably to do with drying time and the volume of clay used, or may be the adaptation of a tile making machine. In the long term this form did not prove useful and most perforated bricks are now perforated only on the bed face.

The first perforated brick making machine was patented by Robert Beart who owned a brickworks at Arlesey in Bedfordshire. He invented a tile machine in 1852 which he adapted for bricks, and also made agricultural land drainage tiles. Beart's patent still applied in 1856 when Humphrey Chamberlain of Kempsey, who had a new brickmaking machine, stated that anyone who made perforated bricks by machine was liable to pay a patent royalty to Robert Beart.[108] Kempsey would have been a logical place to supply bricks for any new building in Great Comberton as river transport would have been much easier for such heavy goods than road. There is also a record of bricks delivered from William Hampton's Brick and Tile

---

107 Clive Richardson, Architect's Journal 6th April 2000
108 Journal of the Society of Arts, Vol 4 no 185 June 6th 1856 www.jstor.org

Works in Apperley to Eckington wharf in 1857 and 1858 for the price of 28s per thousand.[109]

The roofs of the barn and cowshed were originally of slate, which became commercially available from the end of the 18th century, but this had been replaced with corrugated asbestos sheet.

The construction of the cowshed and rebuilding of the barn is probably the work of Elizabeth Whillock, William's widow, who died in 1863 or her son Walter who died in 1875.

In 1997 the barn had an earth floor and once contained a cider mill, the marks where it was fixed to one of the beams can still be seen. Hugh Peart recalls that it was turned by a horse called Katy who was stabled in the southern part of the barn. This would have been where John Hardy made the 9 hogsheads of cider listed in his inventory.

There is a well in front of the Bothy which refills quickly and other in the Farmhouse garden which had been covered over and buried and which was only discovered when BT replaced a telegraph pole and drove the anchor for the stay through the cover. Two water storage cisterns existed, one is under the paving outside the sitting room of the Farmhouse and the other under the corner of the kitchen next to the front door. A large cheese pressing block sat outside the back door in the farmyard and now forms part of the garden wall near the barn.

---

109   BA950 705.85.63

OTHER HOUSES IN GREAT COMBERTON

The map included in four parts after this text is undated but must be about 1815. It shows occupiers not owners. The big yew in the churchyard is the only tree shown so was a notable size then. Russell Street is labelled Great Russell Street and is noted as the road to Evesham. Church Street is identified as the road to Pershore, but as the map was probably drawn by Thomas Collingridge who was then the tenant of Manor Farm, we can't assume this was a more important road than the one further west, it might just have been his route to Pershore. Note the road to the old Quay in a different place to the current Quay Lane, and the road to Plumbden (the location of the present quay) opposite Stowe Cottage.

Pool House, also known as Lay Pool

This is probably the house sold by William Wright to William Wade of Wick in 1704 when it was lately erected and left by him in his will to his brother Robert. Samuel Andrewes owned it in 1798, when it was occupied by Susannah Whillock, and in 1809 it was bought by Cyprian Whillock from Andrewes, and occupied at some point by James Phillips. Allocated at Inclosure to William Whillock in 1820 when the orchard, which was previously owned by Charles Edward Hanford, was allocated to Ann Ricketts. In 1858 William Groves lived there as the tenant of Elizabeth Whillock who left it to her son Walter. Walter's wife Lucy left it to her niece Annie Munslow. The pool on the corner of the road opposite the war memorial was filled in, probably around 1961 when the County Council replaced hedges on corners with iron railings to improve visibility.

Kent's Farm

Kent's Farm was occupied by John Whoods in 1802 and 1815, and owned by Ann Ricketts in 1815 and 1820. It is possible John Whoods was a tenant before 1815 not its owner, and it was occupied by John Jones before that. The orchard which now belongs to Pool House belonged to Kent's Farm along with a block of land along the Mary Brook. There was a large barn along the roadside and a square dovecote next to it, said to have had walls three feet thick and to have 1425 nesting holes, the base of which can still be seen. Both were still there until sometime between 1955 and 1970 according to the Ordnance Survey. Kent's Farm was once a Youth Hostel. There is a tantalising hint, unsubstantiated in the archives, that Kent's Farm may be the original West Green Manor.

Orchard Cottage

The cottage next door to Kent's Farm was owned by John Whoods in 1820, with five fields attached. On the 1815 plan no occupier is shown and it appears to be part of Ann Ricketts's holding

Shelton Farm

Owned by Mr Shelton in 1798 and occupied by John Phillips. William Kermetts was the tenant in 1815, and John Shelton was recorded there in 1815. By 1820 it was owned by Samuel and John Phipps. John Phipps was still there in 1834 but by 1884 it was in the ownership of Mrs Anne George. Shelton Farm included most of the land from the old Pershore Road, and Quay Lane to the river and Lillworth.

Cottage replaced by Avon Rise.

This cottage was demolished by Ralph Brookes in the mid-20th century. William Pugh and Ann Whoods were associated with this house in 1815, probably tenants. T. Butt was shown there in 1809 and in 1820 it was probably owned by Thomas Butt. In 1885 it was shown as a pair of attached cottages. The ownership of this house, Clarke's Cottage and The Thatch in 1820 is not clear. They are within the boundary of the land owned by Joseph Clarke but shown as separate plots.

Clarke's Cottage

Elizabeth Nash lived in Clarke's Cottage in 1815, but she may have been a tenant and not the owner. It was probably owned by Joseph Goodwin otherwise Clarke in 1820, but, in common with the cottages on either side, its ownership is not quite clear.

An indenture of the 14th October 1747 held in the Stowe Cottage deeds in which Francis Drinkwater of Great Comberton, cordwainer, son and heir apparent of William Drinkwater sells William Langston of Great Comberton *all that piece of ground situate and being next adjoining the now (new?) dwelling house of the said Francis Drinkwater in Great Comberton whereon a barn lately stood and was lately pulled down by the said William Langstone who is now building a new tenement or cottage thereon, and also the joint use of a well belonging to the said dwellinghouse of the said Francis Drinkwater, and also all that ground shooting from the lower end of the lower corner of the said dwelling house of the said Francis Drinkwater and from thence down to a certain close called Clarke's Close.* Clarke owned land behind Clarke's Cottage, but also behind Church Cottage and the Old Smithy so this could relate to any of these. However Clarke's Cottage and the house which was replaced by Avon Rise are the only two so closely together from which it is downhill to the land of Clarke.

The Thatch

Thomas Deaves occupied The Thatch between 1716 and 1766, Joseph Mann was there in 1815 and Nancy Mann probably owned it in 1820, but it fell within the boundary of Joseph Goodwin otherwise Clarke's land.

Stowe Cottage

Stowe Cottage was originally the Parish Houses; effectively almshouses, recorded as such in 1815 and as Poor in 1809, with the village pound, where straying animals were corralled, in the front garden. In 1820, like several other properties in the village, its ownership is not clear. It is within the boundary of land owned by T. Moore of Bay Tree Cottage but shown as a separate plot. In 1885 it is shown as a pair of attached cottages. By 1897 it was owned by Edward Smith of Morton House, Childswickham, one of the sons of John Smith. He provided it with a water supply in 1896 and then sold it to his sister Marianne for £115 in 1897. It was occupied by Elijah Stow and Hannah Groves at the time and it was noted that it used to be four tenements.

Pound House

Occupied by R. Lane in 1809, and E. James and Fewtrill in 1815, probably tenants of John Smith who owned it in 1820, along with all the land down to the river and the field now covered by Hand's Orchard.

Next to it was a building listed as Wm Kennetts shop.   In 1885 it was shown as a pair of attached cottages with a small building to the north on the roadside which might have been the shop.

Bank Cottage, previously called Cooke's House.

In 1809 the orchard behind it was labelled Cooks Orchard, and it was occupied by William Sandals in 1815. John Whoods the Elder's will, probate granted 1st February 1793, left a messuage with cyder or perry mill, garden and orchard to his wife Mary for life, then to his grandson William, son of John Whoods Junior. John Whoods owned it in 1820, and transferred to Thomas, his second son, all that dwelling house called Cooke's House formerly in the occupation of William Sandells with garden and orchard. Thomas mortgaged it and then sold it to Henry Hopkins yeoman of Great Comberton in 1837. In his turn he mortgaged it, when it was tenanted by William Simmons and Thomas Whoods. Henry left it to his wife Sarah and his children. His son Gabriel bought out the others in 1888 and finally paid off the mortgage the following year. All these deeds are in the ownership of Stowe Cottage.

Whiteoaks

Whiteoaks is a bit of a puzzle as it appears on the 1809 map but is not shown on the 1820 Inclosure Award plan, although it falls within land allocated to the Reverend L Middleton, so it was owned by the church. In 1815 it formed part of the then rector, Mr Williams's, allocation, and in 1815 Joseph Youngs lived there. John Whoods had the yard behind. On the 1885 OS map the Reading Room is shown attached to the Rectory and noted as the School, although the village scrapbook states that it was built in 1896 funded by public subscription. Whiteoaks is likely to have been the four freehold adjoining cottages which were sold in 1850 and occupied by Thomas Birch, George Richardson and Thomas Futrill with the fourth empty as the census puts those named people nearby.

The Rectory

Shown as the Parson's House in 1815 and occupied by the Rev Thomas Williams, then by the Reverend L. Middleton in in 1820 and subsequently by the Reverend Charles Hubert Parker. There was a barn along the roadside to the south of the house. An unattributed note in the village scrapbook states that the Rectory was built by Charles Hubert Parker between 1826 and 1833 for £4000. Noakes Guide to Worcestershire records that the Rectory is said to have been built by John Masefield's grandfather and that the poet is believed to have stayed at Bank Cottage. Neither has been verified.

Joe's Farm

Occupied by William Hopthings in 1815 and owned by C.J. Halford in 1820, along with the field stretching across to Church Street and land between the Pershore Road and Porter's Cottages.

Stonewell Piece and April Cottage

Mrs Mary Whoods lived here in 1815, and before that John Whoods the elder owned it. In 1836 she left it to her daughter Elizabeth Andrews. In 1884, CH Parker, who had been busy buying up a number of houses in the village, auctioned it. It had been occupied by Matthews, then Matthew Mann and John Whoods and since had been made from 2 into 3 cottages occupied by William Simons, Joseph Mann and James Faulkener. It is evident from old photographs that Stonewell Piece has had its roof raised in the late 19th or early 20th century. Matthew Mann was listed as a beer seller in Bentley's directory of 1840.

Cottage replaced by Waterbrook House

This was a small cottage noted in 1815 as occupied by Thomas Pulley. There appears still to be a building there is 1820 but with a number but with no owner attributed. The 1885 OS map shows a similar layout.

Vine Cottage

Vine Cottage has an almost complete set of title deeds, still in the possession of the owners of the house, from 1757 where it is described as being *lately erected on part of an orchard called Cartwright's* in an indenture of sale from Thomas Hand to William Davis. There is a question remaining over its attribution to Francis Dinely on the 1820 Inclosure Award Plan since William Davis left it to his siblings Edward and Ann. He was probably a tenant. Edmund Smith V, butcher lived there with his 13 children and it was sold by his daughter Lucy Ricketts to Annie Hardy in 1815. As Annie Munslow she sold it to John Reginald Peart and Mrs Peart in 1936.

House on the corner of Russell Street and Church Street replaced by Hand's Orchard.

The site of this house is now occupied by Hand's Orchard. It was occupied by John Jones in 1815 and owned by Lane in 1820. In 1834 John Smith paid 4s chief-rent for Thos. Hands's house which may be this one.

Bay Tree Cottage

Sadly, the old documents which belonged to Bay Tree Cottage were stolen by the previous owners when it was last sold. It was occupied by Thomas Moore in 1815 and owned by him in 1820.

Longacre

Longacre is most likely to be the house Edward Leadon left to his grandson Edmund Smith I in 1695, and remained in the Smith family until at least 1820. On both the Inclosure Award plan and the 1815 plan it seems to be T or L shaped with a cross wing hard up against Church Street, so it would appear to have been substantially altered at various times. There was also a small cottage immediately to its north occupied by Elish. Moore in 1815, which was not shown in 1820. By 1885 it appears that the part of the house along Church Street has gone but the building has extended to the east. The small house to the north was still there, but gone by 1904.

Tibbetts Farm, previously known as Lower Farm

Originally the tithe farm for the Woollas manor and tenanted by James Phillips in 1798 and 1815. In 1820 it was allocated to the Reverend Thomas Williams. In 1844 it was owned by Ann Johnson (formerly Ann Halford) and in 1861 tenanted by Shekell. On the 1st March 1927 Albert Lamas Cresswell bought it from E B Shekell. Walter Revers moved there at Easter in 1938. There is no substance in the popular myth that Shakespeare's lawyer lived here. Thomas Russell (of Strensham and Rushock) was a friend of Shakespeare's who left him £5 in his will. He was also a friend of John Hanford who built Woollas Hall and who reclaimed land from the Crown with a mortgage of £1,500 from Russell. This suggests the development of Russell

Street, then known as Great Russell Street dates from around 1600, named probably in honour of Thomas Russell.

Farm replaced by Neston

Originally a larger farm with a matching barn to that across the road, parts of the floor of which can be still be seen. It was owned by Thomas Dobbs the elder and his wife Margaret in 1654 in 1688 by Thomas Dobbs the younger, his only son. In 1709 it was sold by James and Ann Daunce to Bolter. By 1798 it was owned by William Clemens, noted as late Boulters and occupied by Joseph Mann. William Clemens owned it in 1815 and 1820 and it was then bought by The Reverend Charles Hubert Parker in 1834, who auctioned it in 1884. At that time it was occupied by George Allen and Ann Birch. In 1885 it appears as one long building including the barn with a separate small house to the south-west. The current house postdates this. It was one of the houses in the village with a pigeonhouse.

Fern Cottage

This is most likely to be the house Thomas and Sibill Wright lived in that was left by their great-grandson William to Edmund Smith fisherman. It was owned by John Smith in 1820 but occupied by Mrs Ricketts in 1802 and 1815. In the early 20th Century it was two houses. Mary Ann Smith owned it when she died in 1909 when it was sold by her son for £1105.

Two Farm Cottages

These replaced a pair of cottages owned by Mrs Jobling and occupied by Charles Berry and Ann Birch which burnt down in 1893 due to Mrs Birch overheating the oven for cooking.

The Old Smithy

Occupied in 1815 by John Worvilles, possibly a tenant. In 1820 it was owned by James Clarke, along with all the land around Church House and a field on the south side of Russell Street.

Church House

This was recorded as owned by the Church Wardens in 1820 and consisted of 5 cottages. Thomas Collingridge describes it as Colledge Row (sic) on his 1815 map. It was originally thatched and there is a record of sinking a well in 1862 and rethatching in 1865 in the Parish accounts.[110] It was bought by the Rector, Charles Hubert Parker in 1880 for £256 9s when it was described as five dwellings known as Church Houses and occupied by Edward Mann and others. In 1885 it is shown as a row of three or possibly four cottages.

Church Cottage

This may be the property left by Edmund Smith in 1780 to his wife Ann and then to his son Edmund. It was occupied by William Moore and Mary Finn in 1815. A separate house to the west was occupied by Thomas Whillock. By 1885 it is shown as two houses but as one building. On the other side of Church Street there was an enclosure called Wittons Orchard in 1815.

Westend

This house is not shown on the 1820 Inclosure Award plan or the 1815 plan but is on the 1885 Ordnance Survey map.

Yew Tree House, possibly previously known as Whittons or Ashland

Owned by Mrs Clarke in 1809, D. Clarke in 1815 and shown as Clarke in 1820. It may be the property in the ownership of James Clarke in 1834 when the land tax describes *Mrs Clarkes house what was formerly called Whittons*. James Clarke's will dated the 7th October 1836 splits his property between his daughters Charity Ann Ricketts of Eckington, Theodosia Careless (outright winner of the most-splendid name in the village competition) and Bright Clarke. Clarke is often referred to as *Clarke also Goodwin*. A field lower down Church Street, on the other side of the road was called Whittons Orchard.

Manor Farm

As its name implies this has always been the home farm to Woollas Hall, owned by the Hanfords. In 1719 Edward Roberts held the lease, in 1795 it was occupied by Ann Phillips, with Whoods and Clemens as under-tenants. Thomas Collingridge lived there in 1815 and 1816. Edward Mytton was the tenant in 1851 and 1861.

Cottage A

This is the first of the houses on Back Lane demolished by Ralph Brookes, a timber-framed cottage so substantial that it defied demolition and was burnt down. Before 1820 it was two cottages owned by Ann Ricketts and in 1820 it was allocated to Charles Edward Hanford. E. Hancock and Thomas Birch lived there in 1815 and Brite Clarke in 1851.

Cottage B

Owned by C.E. Hanford in 1820, occupied by S. Heath in 1815, J Timbril in 1815 and 1834, and Thomas Birch.

Cottage C

A small cottage demolished before 1885 in the field known as Heath's Close on the corner between the drive up to Manor Farm and the track which leads to the farm barns. Owned by Charles Edward Hanford in 1820, and occupied by E. Moore in 1815 and Thomas Moore between 1851 and 1861.

Cottage D

Occupied by William Spires in 1815, J. Andrews in 1815, and owned by Fisher in 1820, and by Eleanor Collingridge at some point later.

Cottage E

The last of a row of 4 old cottages working downhill along the north-west side of Back Lane, demolished by Ralph Brookes and replaced with bungalows and semis between 1950 and 1970. Shown on the 1815 plan of the village as occupied by William Fewtrell. Bought by Mary Stanley before 1820 but still occupied by W. Futrill in 1851. Owned by Mrs Whillock in 1858, along with the surrounding orchard, which she had owned since before 1815.

The popular myth about old timber-framed houses is that they were built using ship's timbers. Oliver Rackham, probably the greatest authority in trees and woodlands, says there is no evidence for this, and, if you think about it, the timber required is different – predominantly curved for ships and mainly straight for houses. Added to which, why and how would you transport wood so far when there were woods growing and other reusable timber buildings near at hand. The Court Rolls of Elmley Castle record instances of villagers asking permission to demolish and rebuild houses and barns, and this would more plausibly explain the redundant sockets found in the beams of old houses. A curved timber in Fern Cottage may well have been wind bracing from the castle in Elmley which was falling into ruin at about the time Russell Street was being developed; a similar one is in the bar of the Star Inn in Pershore

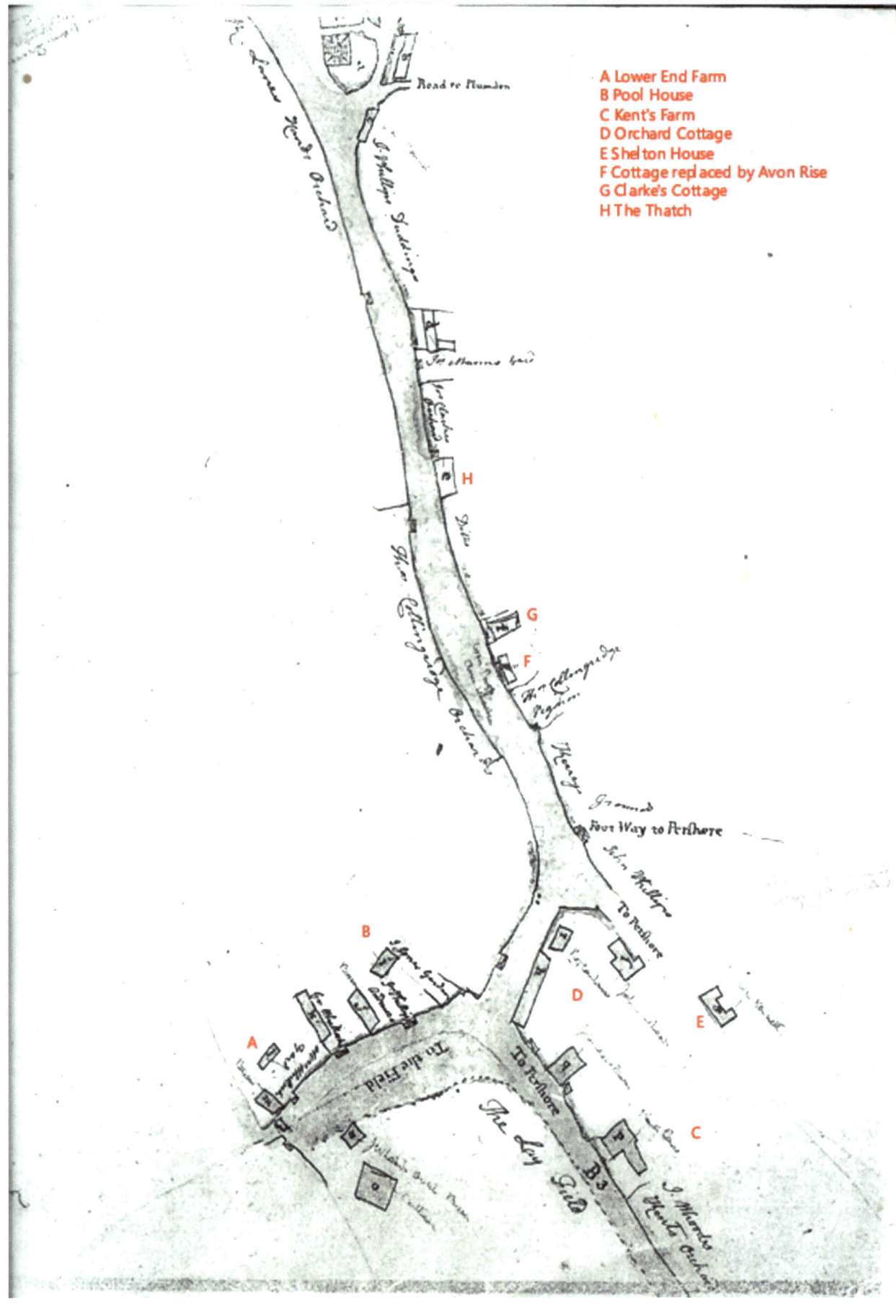

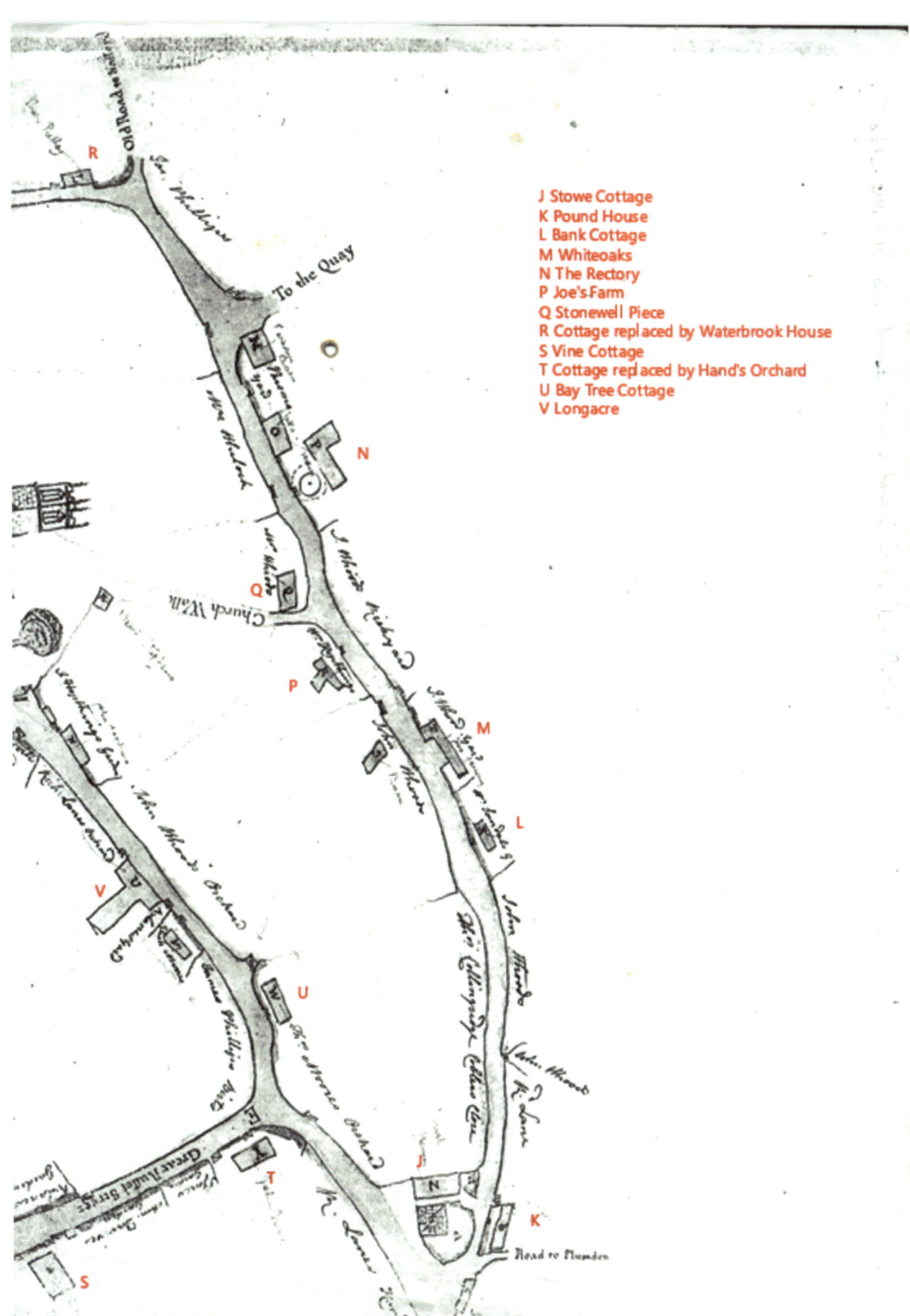

J Stowe Cottage
K Pound House
L Bank Cottage
M Whiteoaks
N The Rectory
P Joe's Farm
Q Stonewell Piece
R Cottage replaced by Waterbrook House
S Vine Cottage
T Cottage replaced by Hand's Orchard
U Bay Tree Cottage
V Longacre

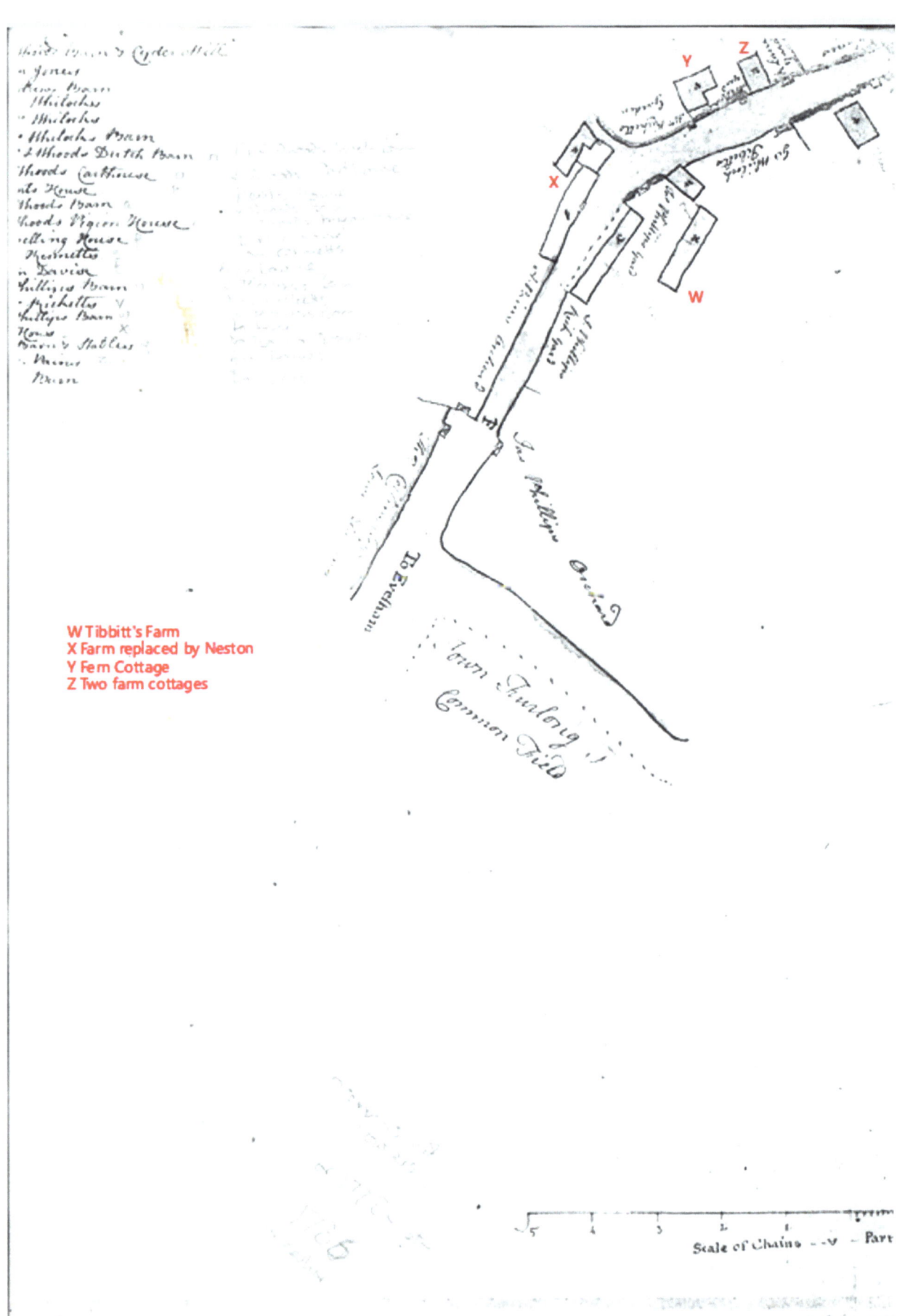

W Tibbitt's Farm
X Farm replaced by Neston
Y Fern Cottage
Z Two farm cottages

Lower End Farm

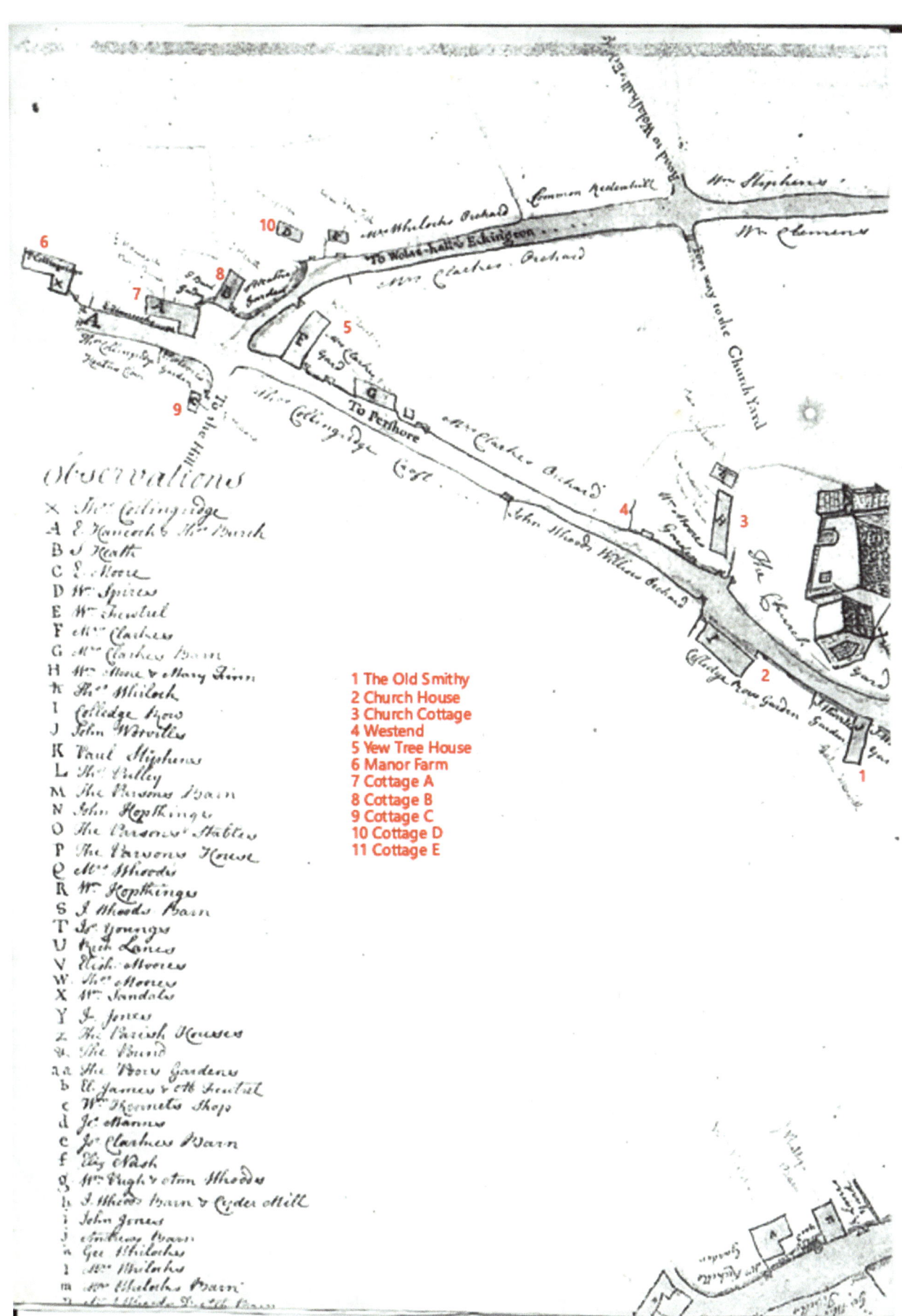

1 The Old Smithy
2 Church House
3 Church Cottage
4 Westend
5 Yew Tree House
6 Manor Farm
7 Cottage A
8 Cottage B
9 Cottage C
10 Cottage D
11 Cottage E

ACKNOWLEDGEMENTS

Many people have generously given time and invaluable information, and my thanks are due to the following:

The staff of the Worcestershire Archaeology and Archive Service at The Hive, Worcester

John Dixon and Wendy Snarey - Tewkesbury Historical Society

David Kitching and Martyn Fretwell - British Brick Society

Chris Holden – Life and Death on the Royal Charter

Chester Subaqua Club

Ian Munro – Fire Services Museum of Victoria

Alan Wadsworth – Worcestershire Farmsteads Project

Birmingham Archives, Heritage and Photography Service (formerly Birmingham City Archives)

The National Archives, Kew

Brian Sinnett

Reg and Lyn Salisbury

Jackie Taylor

www.ingramcontent.com/pod-product-compliance
Lightning Source LLC
Chambersburg PA
CBHW040456240426
43663CB00034B/55